A Loose Herd of Texans

A Loose Herd
of Texans

By
Bill Porterfield

TEXAS A&M UNIVERSITY PRESS

College Station and London

Porterfield, Bill.
    A loose herd of Texans.

    1. Texas–Social life and customs. 2. Texas—
Biography. 3. Porterfield, Bill. I. Title.
F391.P84   976.4'06'0922   77-99277
ISBN 0-89096-044-5

Manufactured in the United States of America
FIRST EDITION

For
Tice Covey Porterfield
Janavee Elizabeth Harrell Porterfield

What I have inherited from you I must
earn over again for myself or it will
not be mine.

Contents

Introduction: A Mythical Place

Texas is still a caricature, damn it.

There is no other way to describe it, try as you might in so short a space. Sure, if one had the pages, not to speak of the power, of a Tolstoy, and the time he took to take us to the steppes of Russia, then one could write of Texas and its people without cliché. Stereotypes which stick in the desert of the mind like prickly pear would soften and surrender to a steady rain of specificity. Panorama would give way to closeup; people and place would come into focus as individual and unique and yet all too human and familiar, and we would glory in the universality, not the rootin', tootin' chauvinism of it all. And yet caricature is appropriate here—the word must match the deed, in outline at least. Texas is an exaggeration, not only of itself but of the American dream, past and present. As old as Indians and cowboys, it is as new as the last moon shot and the latest millionaire. Between those extremes of time, temper, tall tales, and technology, however, lies the truth, the middling mean, about the Lone Star state.

Imagine a mythical region so vast that it contains, universe-like, man's ultimate metaphysical home, Paradise, as well as a half acre of Hell. Well, one is a town in Texas, and the other has been used to designate a brothel in Fort Worth and a Brewster County mountain range. Attend a New World territory so distant and diverse that it held in its bosom ancient Mongolian hordes—eleven Indian tribes—as well as memory of home for ark after ark of European, Asian, and African immigrants. The settlement of Texas was not a private outing restricted to Anglo-Saxons. Every race and almost every nationality came along, laid out towns, and named them after other capitals and countries. In some cases it was a pathetic attempt to conjure up civilization amid rude surroundings: Athens, Carthage, Geneva, Ireland, Italy, London and New London, New Berlin, New Boston, Orient, Nassau, Salem and Old Salem, Stockholm, Trinidad, Vienna, Warsaw, Waterloo. For five hundred years, from the time of the first Spanish explorer to the present, Texas flew under six flags—those of Spain, France, Mexico, the Republic of Texas, the Confederacy, and the United States. This is, of course, not counting the Indian nations, who had their staffs and symbols, too.

The best way to describe the geography of Texas is to take you to the tower of the University of Texas in Austin, just as Professor Clarence Ayres did John Gunther back in the early 1940's. The tower is not all that high, but if you raise yourself in your imagination, your mind can perceive what your guide is telling you. The tower, the city of Austin itself, sits upon the back of a geological fault, a fissure that splits the table of Texas right down the middle, north and south. That fault is called the Balcones Escarpment in polite company. In beer joints it is known as the Devil's Backbone. I have always seen it as the spine of some Texas-sized dinosaur, the beast having been buried standing up in some volcanic eruption eons ago. Whatever, it creates a split personality in the lay of the land. To the east lies the farm country and the shade of woods. It is rolling to flat, a plain of post oak and then pine, a place of rich and fruitful soils, soft and Southern in its sensibilities. It contains most of the towns and cities and most of the population. Many of the state's black people remain in that half. To the west of the fault stretches the ranch country—first the rolling prairie and then the rising High Plains which finally bump into the rump of the Rocky Mountains. Out there it is hot and arid. The towns and cities are few and far between. So, relatively speaking, are people. The closer you get to the Rio Grande and the border, however, the more you realize how much of Mexico is in Texas and its character.

In spite of droughts and the sprawl of urban outposts, in spite of the spread of superhighways and the passing of farm and rural county seat life, in spite of the decline in the number of farms, agribusiness is still the state's leading industry, a production which even outearns oil and other minerals.

And yet Texas remains the preeminent oil and gas producing state of the nation. All this oil has been the fuel that fed the great explosion of manufacturing which took place in Texas in the late thirties and which continues today. It paved the way for the most far-reaching and best-maintained highway system in the United States, roads that brought the rural folk into cities such as Houston, Beaumont, and Port Arthur, the great port and petrochemical triangle on the Gulf Coast.

If Houston was a port, Dallas to the north was a fort, a vault, a cathedral to banking and finance on the forks of the Trinity. Across the river, Fort Worth turned its attention from the withering West to the sky and saw soaring possibilities in manufacturing aircraft. To the south and center of the state, Waco grew as an agribusiness hub, while down on the tail of the dinosaur Austin flourished as the seat of government and education. In Mexican Texas, Old San Antonio braced itself with breweries and military installations. Corpus Christi built itself upon the bay, a navy seaport and petrochemical paradise with balmy skies and breezy palms. Kingsville became more than just the company store for the King Ranch. And Brownsville, at the tip of the border with Mexico, and its sister cities west along the Rio Grande became tourist bazaars and headquarters for citrus plantations—a necklace of nectar.

Around the Big Bend and up into foothills of the Rocky Mountains, El Paso broke through to become sister city to Ciudad Juárez and the largest bilingual border metropolis in the world. Northeast across the Staked Plain and into the High Plains, into the teeth of Panhandle winds and flying tumbleweeds, the cities of Midland, Odessa, Lubbock, and Amarillo took root and held on with cattle and oil, even irrigating for a harvest of wheat. Just east across the Cap Rock Escarpment, Wichita Falls, Abilene, and San Angelo perked up out of the prairie grass, each a hundred miles south of the last and each as prickly in its pride as a cactus flower. The saga of the cities did not stop there. It ran east along the Oklahoma border to the

edge of Arkansas and Texarkana, then dropped to Tyler, Longview, and Marshall, alongside Louisiana.

Between the last three cities and Houston, of course, lay
the piney woods of East Texas, a forest so large that it could hide
outlaws, Southern gothics, and a remnant of Indians in perfect,
if primitive, seclusion. It would come to harbor four national
forests as well as a harvest of riches for lumbermen and oilmen.
There, H. L. Hunt found his bonanza.

Except for a slight recession now and then, none of that
stunning growth has stopped. Alaska and the Arabs to the contrary, Texas remains a colonial outpost gargantuan in size and
resources. It came into being as a colonial mine of great treasure, its landowners and its producers and shippers and manufacturers growing rich and fabled on the products they exported
to the rest of the country and the world. There was no middle-
man class, no managerial carpetbaggers from the east to come
between the boss and the workers. Thus, there were no corporate
bureaucracies and no labor unions. You had the do-it-yourself
entrepreneur on the one hand and the hired hand on the other.
If this created wide disparities in wealth, it also encouraged a
sense, even at the lowest levels of society, that almost anything
was possible if a man could just get a grubstake. That spirit
continues. If you can't get it in oil now, you can get it in com-
puters. Ask Ross Perot or Sam Wylie.

Yet having said this, one must face the fact that Texas is
still, in terms of money and power and class, something of a
feudal state. In spite of its greater democratization, it is yet
ruled by special interests and those they designate to run things,
whether in Austin or Washington. But perhaps this, really, is
the way of the world. What makes Texas such an epic place
within the dream of America is that it is still a happy hunting
ground for the entrepreneur of whatever origin or inclination.
Its greatest wealth, the resource of the land and what it yields,
changes hands among the privileged few instead of the many.
Yet the only arbiter of privilege is money, and almost anyone
can make it if he wants it badly enough.

There are, in round numbers, about twelve million of us,
and I'll cross my heart and hope to burn in hell if you'll see

most of us on a horse or in a Cadillac, except maybe once a year at rodeo time or when some show-off invites us to the country club. It is true that we have horses in Texas—more than ever before—but the one in every forty Texans who owns a horse is way behind the one in every ten Texans who has a pickup truck. But watch your generalizations! This does not mean that every pickup has a rifle rack in the rear window and a citizen's band radio on the dash. Just as it does not mean that every Texan who drives a Cadillac is a millionaire. We do carry guns fairly freely, and we do talk by radio on the road of life, and indigestion knows we love bourbon and beer, barbecue and chicken-fried steak, but it would be inaccurate to hold up the redneck beside the cowboy and the millionaire as a symbol of the new Texas. We are too diverse a people; we simply dwarf, in numbers and subtlety, that exaggerated and grotesque trinity.

Play a game with yourself. What two Texans come immediately to mind? LBJ and John Connally. That's what hit me right off. But other pairs are persistent. H. L. Hunt and Howard Hughes. Larry Mahan and Walt Garrison. Jesse Jones and Amon Carter. Leon Jaworski and Percy Foreman. Stanley Marcus is in a class alone. Barbara Jordan and Anne Armstrong. Larry King and Larry McMurtry. Tom Landry and Darrell Royal. Walter Cronkite and Dan Rather. Willie Nelson and Waylon Jennings. Henry B. Gonzalez and José Ángel Gutierrez. J. Frank Dobie and John Graves. Lee Trevino and Ben Crenshaw. Sarah Hughes and Frances ("Sissy") Farenthold. Davy Crockett and Sam Houston. George Foreman and Duane Thomas. Amarillo Slim and Suckrock Johnson. Dolph Briscoe and Lloyd Bentsen. Lady Bird Johnson and Oveta Culp Hobby. Billie Sol Estes and Ben Jack Cage. Margo Jones and Preston Jones. The list could go on. But what is obvious is that even among the out-sized—those profiles that rise like Rushmores above the Texas plains—there is great variety, certainly enough to dispel the sense of a "reactionary sheikdom"—Chandler Davidson's ironic description—run by loud-mouthed barbarians.

If Texas has more rich, it also has more poor. Rugged individualism is valued over social conscience. It is better to be strong than to be weak, even to be brutal than to be forgiving.

It is still a frontier to challenge the adventurer, and yet already a corporate state super enough to please even an Ayn Rand. It is the last gold rush, the tail end of manifest destiny and the fuse to future shock. No man with gumption would have thought of leaving Texas in the heraldic past, unless he were at gunpoint. There was too much excitement. Hell, a continent had to be explored, a wilderness subdued, the Indians pushed back, and buffalo butchered. Longhorns had to be driven to market, railroads brought in, and oil rigs set in motion.

It was not so long ago, really. You can drive out to the western edge of Fort Worth and look into the setting sun and see in the distance Butch Cassidys riding lickety-split for Hell's Half Acre and a night on the town. The horses' hooves kick up a cloud of white dust in the red sky. Windmills are taller than trees on the horizon. A sonic boom breaks the spell. High in the Western sky, but descending, a 747 out of Los Angeles arcs toward Dallas–Fort Worth airport. Something snaps in you. You give a yahoo and head for Joe T. Garcia's to wash down tamales with a bottle of beer. Reach for a brew, then, and settle back and meet my friends and kin and countrymen.

A Loose Herd of Texans

Uncle John

Uncle John Pierson was an incurable dreamer.

That was the heart of him. The rest of his character grew out of his fantasies, as foisted on his fellow man, which meant that Uncle John had to keep moving to stay ahead of the growing posse of men and women who had set a bounty on his hapless hide. I say hapless instead of ornery because Uncle John wasn't onerous out of ill intent. He meant well even when he wreaked havoc, which was most of the time.

Part of the problem was his charm. At first blush women loved him. He approached young and old with equal gallantry and broke many a heart when they realized he was here today and gone tomorrow. Among men he mixed well. On those small-town sidewalk Saturdays he could be as courtly as a colonel to the promenading ladies and then duck into the pool hall and cue up and casually cuss with the best. And of course he always had a proposition, a little something for everyone, a side deal here and a big deal there. The war was on abroad, and although we weren't in it yet, we were already feeling the pinch of shortage and hearing talk of rationing. If your lady didn't like nylons, Uncle John could get her silk. In a dry county he knew the bootleg, in a tight country the black market.

It was just such a spirit of shady enterprise that brought Uncle John into our lives early in 1941. You see, he didn't belong to us by blood. Daddy brought him home from the pool hall one day, all aglow with liquor and the likelihood that at last, after all the years of living from payday to payday, we were about to come into a small fortune. Daddy went directly to his closet and brought out his only inheritance—a fiddle from his father, a red little jewel that grandfather had inherited from his father.

Grandpa Porterfield had been a stern and patriarchal farmer who thrashed and worked his kids when they were rambunctious. At dusk, however, when they were milk-sopped and subdued, he softened and played them ballads and jigs on the fiddle. Out of all the boys, Daddy had gotten the violin because he was the only one willing to fiddle with it. Now that his own square dance–calling days were over, it lay in its case in the closet, gathering neglect. One day I had come home from school convinced that Grandpa's fiddle was worth more than sentimental value. I had been reading in an encyclopedia about the great Italian violin maker, Antonius Stradivarius. Wasn't that the name carved into the pegboard of Grandpa's instrument? Daddy got it out. It was true! The paper inside matched the Stradivarius label that had been in the encyclopedia. A true Stradivarius would be worth thousands. Was it possible?

"I don't know," Daddy had said. "All I know is that Dad always said this fiddle was older'n he was."

"Well, let's check her out," I had urged, but Daddy squelched me quickly.

"Don't be crazy, boy! We can't claim nuthin Eye-talian right now with old Mussolini joined up the way he is with Hitler and Hirohito."

Daddy's word was law. Still, none of us could resist, from time to time, bragging about our masterpiece. Apparently John Pierson had gotten the full treatment from Daddy at the pool hall. Now, looking back on it all, remembering the expression in John's face when he took up the fiddle, perhaps it had been the other way around. For John Pierson was eloquent. We *had* a Stradivarius! No doubt about it! He looked at it lovingly, as though it were alive, a fine, long-lost friend and he the connoisseur. He ran his fingers along its lines, held it to the light, and plucked its strings. He sniffed the varnish and tapped the wood, noting the detail of design. He explained to us why it was not an Amati or a Guarnerius or a Guadagnini or a Bergonzi and why it was not a copy. Beyond a doubt, a Strad! There were only

540 of them in the world. No telling what we could get if we handled it shrewdly, and of course, John was the man for the job, our agent, as it were.

He tightened the strings, put the fiddle to his chin, and drew the bow across the gut. Ah! The big warm tones. Unique to the master. He was almost tempted, he whispered, to play his own concerto upon it.

"Play," he was urged. "Play a little of your own music."

"No," he sighed. "It has been so many years I forget Pierson. Beethoven I know better."

He swung into what he said was the D Major concerto, but then stopped abruptly, for Daddy was on his feet hushing him.

"Don't play no German music!" the old man shouted. "Good God, John, we're just about at war with them!"

"I am very rusty," John said impatiently, "so it's just as well. I abuse both the work of the German and the instrument of the Italian."

After that performance John Pierson was the star boarder at our house. He stayed a week, fattening up on Mother's cooking and drinking Daddy's medicinal whiskey for his coughs. We all competed for him. Daddy wanted John to join him out in the boondocks on some drilling rig floor; John, of course, diplomatically declined. He did show up at school one afternoon, to my delight, when we were jock deep in P.E., and stunned us all by clearing the high jump at six feet. If we had had the father and son banquet then, I would have preferred Pierson to Pa, but that treat never presented itself. I did get him to Cub Scouts one afternoon, but most of the time he remained at home with Mother, helping with the meals and housework and fixing things around the place that Daddy hadn't gotten around to. He trimmed the trees and repaired the washing machine wringer, all the while keeping Mother company.

He gossiped with her in a way Daddy never did, complimented her every other minute, did her hair, of all things, and crowned the week by accompanying Mother and me to church, where he somehow convinced Brother Reid to take a respite while he, John Pierson, a pool-playing, profane drifter, delivered the damndest sermon we had ever heard. It was in the form of a eulogy to his dear departed mother. He took the story of Sodom and Lot's wife and transformed sodium chloride into a metaphor for Christian virtue. His mother, he said, was the salt of the earth. That was the highest accolade he could think of to bestow on a mortal Christian. Mrs. Pierson may not have been a saint, but who among us was? We were all frail, yea, below Jesus. But by God, his mother was salty!

"Now if the Salt has lost its saving power," he shouted, "it is good for nothing but to be cast out, trodden under the feet of men! But my mother was good, Christian salt, and she did not lose her saving power."

Every child of God was a lump of salt. Every time you prayed, you salted somebody. Every song you sang, you salted someone. Every home you visited, you salted a sick one. Mrs. Pierson went all over her county sprinkling salt.

Now, natural salt killed insects and snakes. Epsom salt killed infection. Spiritual salt, friends, spiritual salt killed sin! That was the message his mother was sending us from the grave. Get out and sprinkle a little salt on someone. He made it a sing-song. Sprinkle a little salt on someone. Brother Reid sang it. We all sang it. The church house shook under our stamping feet, and in our hearts and above our hymning heads haloes shone.

Monday, Mother went down to the bank and borrowed one hundred dollars and gave it to John.

Daddy's enthusiasm for John began to pale, and he said as much in a subdued, troubled way, but Mother wouldn't hear it. She packed the old man off to work, and then, as she drove me to school, we dropped John out on the highway, suitcase in one hand and fiddle case in the other. He would thumb his way to Chicago, where a Greek he knew would find a big-time buyer to relieve us of the Stradivarius.

Uncle John never made it to Chicago. He sent periodic postcards from places like Earline's Truck Stop in Evening Shade, Arkansas. That's on Highway 167 between Bald Knob and Thayer. The reason I know is because Daddy traced it on the map, his big finger angry and shaking like a guy wire in the wind. He wanted John Pierson's neck, and he wanted his fiddle back. Mother never said a word, but I noticed she began putting extra sweets in Daddy's lunch sack, and she took to rubbing his back at night. We got several cheery notes from Evening Shade because John had fallen in love with Earline. Daddy seemed to forgive him and even laughed at his cards.

Next we heard from John that summer. He was back in Texas, without Earline, running Captain John's Cowboy Village on Highway 71 between Smithville and La Grange, kind of a miniature frontier town tourist attraction. Well, knock off the last two words. Hardly any tourists were attracted. We drove to see him one Sunday. Mother and I thought his place was kind of cute. He had cigar store Indians grouped around some tin tepees, and he sat whittling in front of a Roy Bean–like shack, wearing an old cavalry uniform. He'd bought department store dummies and had dressed them up like cowboys and Lily Langtrys, and they were inside with what-nots he had for sale—the kind of junk you now see in Stuckey's.

Daddy showed a great interest in the merchandise until it dawned on us that what he was looking for was his fiddle.

But Pa never brought it up, I guess because he felt as sorry for Uncle John as Mother and I did. John was only charging a dime to see the whole village, but nobody stopped that day. We sat out front sipping lemonade and listening to the bugs frying. We counted thousands. The sun was so hot it melted the asphalt in the road, and grasshoppers would stick in it and scald. John had a radio in the window, and even that which came from it was depressing.

FDR that very day had returned from a secret shipboard meeting in the North Atlantic with Winston Churchill, and the networks were full of war talk. No way we could stay out of it, Daddy guessed. Hell, the Germans occupied the Balkans, the Netherlands, most of Scandinavia, and France, and now they were blitzing the British. The Japs were in the Pacific and most of China and Indochina and were aiming at the Philippines and the East Indies. We were all up on our strategic geography in those days, but none of us would have dreamed that at that very moment Japanese aircraft carriers were sailing boldly toward Pearl Harbor.

Mother shuddered and turned the dial to some music.

> Now the Rawlson is a Swedish town,
> The Rillerah is a stream,
> The brawla is the boy and girl,
> The Hut-Sut is their dream. . . .

"I'll swan," Mother sang through her nose. "I can't for the life of me figure out what that means."

"Some war code," Uncle John said glumly.

Daddy scratched his head.

"I'll tell you this," Uncle John said emphatically, a new resolution stirring him. "I'm tired of watching grasshoppers die out there on that sorry excuse for a highway."

"There ain't much traffic," Daddy agreed.

"And what there is isn't giving me the time of the day," Uncle John went on. He shook his head and grinned. "It's all going to Miss Jessie's down there past the railroad trestle."

"You talkin' about the Chicken Ranch?" Daddy whispered, eyeing Mother to see if she was onto them, which she wasn't.

"I could've sworn I saw the governor out there the other day," John said.

"You mean Coke or Pappy?"

"Naw, not Coke. Pappy. Least it looked like him."

It didn't surprise me at all that the governor, or rather the new U.S. Senator from Texas, would be hanging around a chicken farm, if indeed Uncle John was right, which he probably wasn't. But it made sense to my adolescent imagination. Why, Wilbert Lee O'Daniel, or Pappy Lee, as we called him, was the kind of country boy who was more at home among hayseeds than he was among the high-muckety-mucks that hung around the statehouse up the road in Austin. I could just see Pappy and the Light Crust Doughboys out at the Chicken Ranch, stroking their fiddles and selling Hillbilly Flour to beat the band, singing,

> Chicken in the breadpan scratching up the dough,
> Mama in the kitchen saying, "No, child, no."

On the way home that night we crossed the Colorado River so many times I thought we were circling back on ourselves. Daddy grew glum in the gloom, and now and then I would hear him stomp the floorboard of the Terraplane Hudson and swear. He had let Uncle John off the hook on the whereabouts of Grandpa's fiddle, and now it was haunting him. Someday, Daddy swore, he would settle with John, one way or another. In the meantime, we were not to mention his name.

The old man's resolve lasted little more than three months. December came with a double-barreled clout. First word came from the family farm in Oklahoma that Granny was dying, and so in spite of gas rationing and retread tires, Mother and Daddy took off for the badlands, leaving me behind to take the Continental Trailways to Uncle John's for the holidays. He had given up on his cowboy village and was running a service station down at Sarita, which was one gas pump and four Mexican shacks on the highway between Kingsville and Raymondville, in deep South Texas.

It occurred to me as I got off the bus that Uncle John seemed to set himself at many a crossroad in life, but never at a crowded one. It was so quiet out there you could hear the highline wires humming all the way to the Mexican border. The Pierson Petroleum Company was the last gas stop for eighty-nine miles, and it was eighty-nine miles of lonesome country, nothing but mesquite and cactus and rattlesnakes and a thirsty cowpoke or trucker now and then.

Uncle John greeted me with the news that Pearl Harbor had been bombed by the Japanese, and we hung by the radio listening to the war news for a week. Granny hung on, too, for dear life, and kept Mother and Daddy up in Oklahoma for what seemed like the duration. Uncle John enrolled me in the all-Mexican one-room school taught by Rosa Cardenas, and while I learned Spanish, the country mobilized with a patriotic fervor.

There would be no siesta for Sarita as long as Major John Pierson guarded the home front. He organized himself and the four Mexican families into what he thought was a crack civilian defense outfit, and every night he went from door to door checking to see that the eight lights were dimmed and the sixteen curtains closed. He wore a hard hat with insignia and trained his eyes upon the skies for enemy aircraft. Why he thought anyone would bomb Sarita, I can't imagine, and what he and José and Jiminez and Jesús would have done about it is the fantasy of a fine comic novel I'll never get around to writing. Suffice it to say they went around saluting each other until even the women were sick of it.

The trip to Granny's bedside turned into a year's vigil for my folks, with Daddy doing the farm chores and Mother nursing our matriarch. I lived for their letters and the *Saturday Evening Post* that came in the mail with the war news. The advertisements were as inspiring as the features, full of war fever and slogans, and the old jingo Uncle John loved them. He drove a Nash car, and the Nash Kelvinator ads were so stirring, in a martial way, that Uncle John would stiffen and almost salute as we read them: "Peacetime makers of automobiles and refrigerators. Now devoted 100 percent to the job of making America Supreme in the air." Elsie the Borden cow would say, "What's a war without shortages?" and Uncle John would not take cream or sugar in his coffee. He drank R.C. Colas with a passion because they featured in their ads patriots on the homefront— women who were plane spotters, shoemakers who made boots for paratroopers. Surely, someday, the R.C. Cola man assured us, Uncle John would make the roll call. In the meantime, Uncle John gave special attention to Studebaker cars that came into the station, gave them a little extra service because "for the sixth time since 1852, Studebaker was supplying transports for the Armed Forces."

Ma Bell was saying, "Please don't call long distance this Christmas."

"Stout-hearted, shot to hell, but heading home," was the Bendix Aviation motto.

And the war plants implored their workers on with this cry: "A slowdown may mean bare hands against bayonets!"

It was a strange time, when love and hate fought for possession of your heart. One general, I think it was McNair, was quoted as saying, "We must lust for battle; our object in life must be to kill. There need be no pangs of conscience, for our enemy has lighted the way to faster, surer, crueler killing."

And then your heart would melt at something like General Electric's Christmas message of '42: "Christmas is a light no war will dim. It glows in the heart of every man in the armed forces of the United States; it glows in the hearts of those who gather scrap, who use less sugar and coffee and tea and meat, who walk to save gasoline and tires, who keep on buying more war bonds."

It was during the fall of '43 that Uncle John, in a cagey burst of patriotism, made a decision that would cost him and the Pierson Petroleum Company dearly. He decided to give a break on gas to all the boys in uniform and to sell any GI Joe or fly-boy or whatever a fill-up at cost during the month of March. Within the confines of Sarita it seemed a safe enough gesture which Uncle John crowed about. He figured to get a lot of mileage out of it. Hell, the nearest military installation we knew anything about was in Corpus Christi, fifty miles up the coast, and you never saw any of the sailors as far out in the brush as we were. Occasionally you'd see a youngster in uniform hitch-hiking, but that was about it. Well, the first day Uncle John put his bargain boast on the line with a big banner, we had to hire Jesús La Parra to help pump gas. Military men seemed to come out of the chaparral faster than roadrunners. Stacked up ten cars deep in the driveway. Unbeknownst to us, Uncle Sam had slipped into Kingsville and had, almost overnight it seemed, thrown up a naval air station. To make matters worse, some of the ROTC boys from A&I College were suiting up to make the run out our way. Uncle John could not go back on his promise of gasoline to six hundred servicemen without ringing up a penny of profit. It amounted to a loss of more than one thousand dollars, not counting the piddling amount he paid Jesús for his help that month. In a marginal operation like the Pierson Petroleum Company, such a loss seemed insurmountable. Uncle John had to act decisively, and he did.

Aside from a good rain and a cold beer, he reasoned that what that country most wanted was a good-looking, traffic-stopping woman who would take on all comers. One day he went to San Antonio and came back with Ya-Ya del Barrio. She was a sexy little thing, especially within the context of Kenedy County. Uncle John put her up in a little pink shack behind a board fence behind the gas station, and pretty soon the airmen and the college boys from Kingsville were wearing ruts all around the place. It was late in the spring, after the rains when the Christweeds were wet with their bloody blooms, before the word worked itself up to Oklahoma and Mother. I'm guessing it was my teacher, Mrs. Cardenas, who saved me from sin. All I knew was that one day I was on the bus to Oklahoma, where the mention of Uncle John's name was a crime.

Daddy told me later that Uncle John had gone out of business in Sarita and had been transferred to Huntsville. Of course I knew that Huntsville was home of the state prison. And I worried for a while. But then I forgot John. After all, puberty was launching a pimply and full-scaled assault on my adolescence just about the time the war in Europe and Asia was winding down. Granny survived—yet survives!—and we finally got back to Texas.

Then one day a letter came from the prison. Uncle John was dead. He had gotten the October flu while announcing at the prison rodeo, and it had developed into pneumonia. He had scribbled a last note to my dad. It went:

Tice, the collector who has your fiddle is John Cokinis on State Street in Chicago. He's holding it in your name, having tried to sell it all these years. You can get it back by writing him. It looks like he isn't having much luck selling it. I'm not having much luck myself. Good fortune to you and Janavee and Billy Mack, and remember me kindly, if you can.

Affectionately, John

Daddy wrote for the fiddle and got it back, in better shape than it had been before. Cokinis apparently had kept it oiled and tuned all that time. Now Daddy put it back in the closet to remain silent and gather dust.

I grew up, somewhat, and became a newspaperman, and found myself, seventeen years later, working in Chicago for the *Daily News*. One afternoon I looked up John Cokinis. State Street was not stately where the old Greek kept his shop. You would expect to find Maria Lott, the storefront masseuse, or the House of Crazy Tacos there, but what concertmaster in his right mind would go shopping in Cokinis's for a Stradivarius? The truth was that not many had, and that was why John lived in the back and counted his pennies and ruefully admitted that his fiddles, which he had spent a lifetime collecting, had become a bittersweet burden.

"It is a great irony, no?" he said. "Here I have a treasure in Italian masterpieces—twelve Stradivarii, three Guarnerii, a Guadagnini, two Bergonzi—about thirty rare violins in all, worth perhaps two hundred thousand dollars—and I can't sell them. I have to repair cheap fiddles and sell guitars to pay the rent."

He reached into the safe and brought out a fiddle case. He opened it carefully, as if it were a delicate hope chest. Then from a bed of faded blue velvet he lifted out the instrument and held it to the light.

"This is a Stradivarius," he said reverently. "Notice the golden yellow of the wood, the lovely grace of its lines. Very old this, and listen to it sing!"

He bowed the strings.

"You hear? The big warm tones? Unique to the master!"

"Play," I urged him. "Play something."

"My concerto?" he asked.

"Yours? Of course, yours!"

"Ah," he sighed, "It has been so many years I forget Cokinis. Beethoven I know better."

He swung into the D Major concerto, but stopped.

"I am very rusty," he said impatiently. "I abuse both the work of the German and the instrument of the Italian."

I smiled, remembering the other John, and left.

Dallas, 1975

Clarence of Green Mansions

The most interesting man in the capital city is not the governor. Nor is it the University of Texas football coach. Messrs. Connally and Royal, hero types to most Texans, come out dull and one-dimensional when placed beside the self-illuminating body about to be introduced here. Of course, in the scheme of things the trio would never meet, our hero being the odd man out, but not the lesser for it.

His name is Clarence Lee Felter. He is seventy-nine years old, and he lives in a thicket on an otherwise tamed and civilized street in west Austin. Clarence shares his one-room shack with three dogs and a parakeet. No one else is allowed inside. Clarence, however, is not a hermit. He needs people and, he reports proudly, people need him.

The other day, for instance, Clarence noticed garbage collectors were about to haul away a rug a neighbor had discarded. It seemed to Clarence a perfectly good rug, suitable for his house.

"Boys," he called to the garbage men, "Will you leave it? I'm coming with my wheelbarrow."

When Clarence went to pick it up he found that the men had shaken it out and had folded it neatly for him.

"I am a scavenger," he says brightly, giving the word a connotation of adventure and discovery. "You should see the things I turn up in the trash piles. Such treasure!"

Clarence claims he hasn't bought anything in twenty-two years, and you are inclined to believe him. The grounds about his shack are stacked with the litter of his foraging, the rubbish of others in which Clarence sees some final, redemptive use.

The garden hose can be patched, the pot can be plugged, and the old magazines can bear thumbing through one more time. A table can stand with one leg gone, and a cracked mirror can show you yourself. All is junk and old iron, scraps and bits and pieces, odds and ends, the waste and leavings of man and machine. It does not offend Clarence to have to tinker with such stuff. He considers its restoration an exercise in intelligence and creativity as well as frugality.

The neighborhood is full of widows and university students. The widows bring him their dead husbands' clothes, and the students? Well, you know how often they change apartments. Clarence says he has grown fat on the instant potato and minute rice mixes the students throw away by the boxfuls during moves. He has also grown wise on the books they cast out. The latest edition to his library is a soggy but intact edition of *Freud: His Dream and Sex Theories.*

In return, Clarence is a good neighbor, handy with his hands. Last spring a high school girl came to him with a problem. What could she make and sell at the school carnival? "That's an easy one, my dear," Clarence said, and sent her down to Shoal Creek to dig buckets of mud. The girl was properly skeptical until Clarence showed her how to make clay pendants out of the mud. They dried them in the sun, painted designs upon them, and strung them for wearing around the neck. With Clarence hawking them from a booth, the class made a nice profit.

Clarence has even deeper talents, which, on occasion, have aroused the suspicions of the Austin police. During any week, you could observe, if you had the time and inclination, that many people drive up and disappear into the thicket surrounding Clarence's shack. Most are women.

God knows what the police think, but all Clarence is doing is telling fortunes and giving free spiritual advice. But that is no little thing, is it? Clarence is, indeed, an unusual man. Who would think, for example, that this creaking old miser with the instincts of a pack rat was once the inspiration for a Booth Tarkington play, or that in another life he was Timaeus, a Greek sage teaching numbers in the time of Plato?

Tarkington seems almost as far removed from the times as Timaeus, but at least his part in Clarence's life can be authenticated. It is a fact that from 1906 to 1911 Clarence was the stage manager for Tarkington's play *Man from Home*, which ran and ran, first from New York's Astor Theater and then on road shows throughout the Midwest. And it is a fact that in 1919 Tarkington wrote a play entitled *Clarence*, which our hero says was inspired by his example. Perhaps it is so. Tarkington built a career writing about boys, and Clarence was but a boy of seventeen when he joined the *Man from Home* company.

He was as unusual then as he is now.

Clarence first saw the light of day in Austin on October 17, 1889. The date is very important to him. Clarence is an astrologer and thinks it is significant that he was born a Libra, under the seventh sign of the zodiac. He says he was always a sensitive child, attuned to nature and the supernatural as well as to other people. His mother died when he was young, and Clarence took over the cooking and housekeeping chores for his father and elder brothers. He says he took to these tasks quite naturally because in other lives he had been a weaver and dyer and a chef. He grew his hair long, and when his father objected on the grounds that he looked "odd and different," Clarence replied, "Yes, Father, but it is because I am odd and different."

Clarence was a 1902 dropout. He never got beyond the seventh grade. "I knew all they had to teach instinctively," he reminds us. "Remember, I was teaching numbers in 340 B.C."

Anyway, he went off to New York to make his mark, and he did quite well. After five years with Tarkington, he became an actor, singer, and director. He played in the Brady Company's *Little Women* production, worked and directed in stock and repertory groups in Canada, sang in the chorus of comic operas, and, when that kind of work was scarce, performed tricks of magic in night clubs, told fortunes, and sold real estate and advertising.

The scavenger years were yet to come. In those days Clarence lived well. After all, he had a wife, Eileen, and a son and daughter to support. Their life together seems to have been unusual, to say the least. Clarence and Eileen were cousins and, according to Clarence, shared gifts of extrasensory perception. If he was a warlock, she was a witch. They studied the rites and alchemy of the ancients, polished up on mythology, and went off to California to establish a new religion.

"It was to be based upon the teachings of the Tibetans," Clarence recalls. "Unfortunately, I didn't know anything about it and had to drop the idea. Instead, I got interested in Hinduism. I ran into this Indian, Diva Ram Sekul, who was peddling Ridgeway tea. We were living in San Diego then, and I invited him to stay in our home for as long as he liked. I thought I could pick his brain about the Hindu bunk. But you know, he never divulged anything about his religion. I found myself doing all the talking. He left one day, and six months later I read that he was teaching Hinduism to a group of ladies. I monitored the class and discovered that he was telling them the same thing I had told him in our conversations."

The year 1946 found Clarence and Eileen speeding toward Texas in their Oldsmobile. They were both nearing sixty years of age and were weary of chasing every occult fad. Their children were grown and away.

It was time for them to settle down. Clarence's grandfather had left him two acres on Austin's west side. Clarence stopped at a house on Mohle Drive to inquire about his property across the street. A woman came to the door. She was a Mrs. Nitchsky, wife of a potato chip salesman.

"Don't ask me about that crazy old man up in Canada or California, wherever he is," Mrs. Nitchsky said. "Everybody wants to buy the lot, but he won't sell. He lets it grow into a thicket, and he won't pay his taxes."

"Allow me the pleasure of introducing him," Clarence said politely.

Eileen died six months later, and Clarence was left alone in the thicket.

But no, he says he is not alone.

"My wife has passed on from the physical body," he reminded, "but she is not gone. You remember, I am a medium. I feel her presence. She tells me when to take a bath, what to cook, all the things a wife is supposed to do. I talk to her and one of my dead brothers all the time. 'Honey,' I say, 'I hate to bother you, but where did I put my glasses?' 'Where you left them yesterday,' she says, 'in the icebox.' "

Clarence also talks to the trees and plants in his garden. He coaxes a broken Spanish dagger to grow with warm words. He curses the poison ivy until it wilts.

And he astounds all who came to see him.

Last week a novelist, Robert German, dropped in to take the old man's measure.

"What's your dog's name?" German asked casually.

"Galatea," Clarence boomed, raising his shaggy eyebrows. He stared at German. "Know what that's from?"

"A myth, isn't it? The statue brought to life. . . ."

"Aha! A scholar!" Clarence roared. He grabbed German's arm.

"Now tell me, if you can," he challenged, "who was the maiden abducted to the underworld?"

German frowned. "Persephone," he said.

Clarence's jaw dropped in mock surprise.

"Brilliant," he thundered. "Now. Who was her abductor?"

"Pluto?"

"And Persephone's mother . . . ?"

"Ceres," German declared, matching Clarence's boom.

Clarence jumped up and down.

"And the giant with the eye in the middle of his forehead?"

"Polyphemus."

"And the sailor who put out that eye, the hero he tried to kill, was . . . ?"

"Ulysses!"

Clarence cackled.

"Marvelous! And what of his beautiful bride? She had to wait more than ten . . . it was how many years?"

"Twenty, of course!"

Clarence nodded sagely. "And what was her name and what task was she performing?" He was right up in German's face now.

"Penelope, and she was . . . uh . . . knitting?"

"No!" Clarence shouted. "Knitting? Ha! She was weaving!

Correct me if I'm wrong! Ha! Knitting indeed! What was she weaving?"

"Her wedding dress?"

"Dear me, no!" Clarence corrected, pretending to be downcast. "It was a shroud for her father-in-law, Laertes."

German grinned in surrender, and Clarence embraced him.

"After we started, I knew I would lose," German said. "It was just a matter of time."

"Clarence is wonderful," Rev. Charles Howe, pastor of the Unitarian Church of Austin, said later. "He is our most faithful member, and our most vociferous in the public affairs forum. He always has something to say, probably because there is not a philosophical or religious question that he has not tackled at some time or other. His erudition continues to amaze me."

"But why?" Clarence wanted to know. "I've had more than two thousand years' head start on the rest of you."

Austin, 1969

J. D. and the Gang in
The Grove

J. D. Graham's general store looked like one of those lost little places Bonnie and Clyde used to hit back in the thirties. There was a gasoline pump out front full of high-octane cobwebs, a row of old men lounging on the porch, and not enough money in the cash register to bother about. This, of course, was a reflection against Miss Parker and Mr. Barrow and not Mr. Graham. If The Grove settlement was flourishing, J. D., being a competent storekeeper, would have been ringing up dollar signs. But it wasn't and J. D. wasn't.

He sat there, a large, gentle-faced man with red ears and a robust belly, swatting dirt daubers and selling red soda pop and white soda crackers to first one kid and then another. That didn't take long, because there weren't but seven children (and fifty-seven adults) left in The Grove, which is in the Leon River valley between Gatesville and Temple.

I say "left" because to hear J. D. tell it, The Grove used to be a place to be reckoned with. E. C. Symm and W. J. Dube operated general stores, Old Man Johnson had a café, that fella Durham ran a candy kitchen, there was a mule barn run by Mr. Glass, Holcombe and Adams were blacksmiths, Proft and Taylor were the barbers, and Collins and Denman were the doctors. And there were enough residents behind those commercial fellows almost to win over the county courthouse from Gatesville. "We lost by one vote," J. D. said, and you could tell it still rankled him.

Except for the Lutheran Church, J. D.'s was the only place of business left. Some of the other buildings were standing, but there was a gray shimmer of yesteryear about them. Only a drunken ghost could have negotiated the sagging stairway to the doctors' second-story office.

"Odd of you to say that," J. D. said, unfurling an eyebrow that had gone from red to white. "The last man to navigate those steps was an old feller by the name of T. B. Durham. He moved up there after the doctors left. Stayed drunk all the time. Used to fire boilers at the gin. Drunk all the time. Never understood why he didn't break his neck on those stairs."

"What happened to him?"

"Oh, he got sick and died."

J. D. said he guessed the village got sick and died of neglect. After they lost the courthouse fight, the state built Highway 36 around them instead of through them. And then, to make matters worse, the federal government came in at the beginning of World War II and bought up 322 square miles of prime farmland to the west and built Fort Hood. "We lost our big farms," J. D. said. The military base made thriving towns out of places like Gatesville, Copperas Cove, Killeen, and Belton, but it didn't do a thing for The Grove except to obscure it further.

E. C. Symm closed his store, and W. J. Dube sold his. Old Man Johnson closed his café and died. It got to where a business failure was a prelude to a funeral. Durham, the candy kitchen man, closed up and died, and so did Mr. Glass, the mule barn operator, and the two blacksmiths. But they were old anyhow. The younger fellows moved to other towns.

One barber went to Port Arthur, and the other went to Gatesville. Nobody remembers where the doctors went.

J. D. was one of the farmers who found himself without a place to plow. So in 1944 he bought the store from Jim Gilbert, who had bought it from W. J. Dube. August Schkade was running the store alone until Dube went into partnership with him in 1908. Schkade died in 1910, and Dube married his widow.

The store is so old no one remembers its beginning. It might be as old as the well out front, which Uncle Jim Whitmore dug with a pick and crowbar in 1872. The first twelve feet were almost solid rock. The Grove sits right at the flinty edge of the river valley. The well still gives up sweet water, and the wood stove and the big wall clock in the store are almost as durable. The stove has been burning wood and tobacco juice and warming backsides and shoe leather for about seventy-five years, and the clock hasn't stopped ticking since W. J. Dube first wound it in 1910.

It is a handsome instrument, encased in a rich wood cabinet. On its face is the legend, "Linz Brothers Jewelers, Dallas." The four Linz brothers were from Austria. They started out selling diamonds by horse and buggy in Grayson County, north of Dallas. Then they opened stores in Sherman and Denison. By 1898 they were in Dallas in the Linz Building, which for years was the tallest building west of the Mississippi—twelve stories, made of marble. In those days an item from Linz was considered something to strut about, and Dube remembers he got the clock as a premium for selling a lot of something— what, he can't recall.

They peddled a good eight-day clock. W. J. Dube is a man of unswerving habit, and he began winding his every Saturday morning at 5:00, the hour he opened the store. Habit became tradition with Gilbert and now Graham. J. D. figures the clock has lasted as long as it has because its gears have never had to fret.

"It knows just what to expect," he explained. "If I got mixed up and wound it on any other morning than Saturday, it would probably come unsprung and fall off the wall."

But things do not self-destruct in The Grove. They rust and dry rot. Built-in obsolescence is as unknown as smog and riots. Hinges and habit hang on for dear life, and the faces of the men on the porch of J. D.'s store are as stubborn and set in their wrinkled way as their overalls and boots. Is it atrophy or conviction? Surely they vote like creaking gates swinging backwards, and stand for some things best forgotten, and yet it does not matter. Theirs are the faces of a lost America, which, perhaps only because of its passing, seems precious now.

The Lutheran Church bell could have been tolling as much for the town as for the funeral of Mrs. Bertha Winkler Hohle, who had died two days before at the age of seventy-six. Yet even in its wake, in its dozing slide to oblivion, there was an illusory sense of permanence about The Grove, and it centered in the general store.

J. D. remained in The Grove because he belonged there. He was born there, and so were his father and his grandfathers. His maternal grandfather, Abram Wyatt, had brought the mail in from Round Rock by pony express. His paternal grandfather, W. J. Graham, had run the general store that Symm later took over. A hicky looking fellow in a funny hat strolled into the store one day, and W. J. and some of the other men began to pick at him. "Hold on, by God!" the stranger growled, putting his back against the bar and facing them. "Do you fellows know who you're talking to? This is Sam Bass!"

"You could've heard a pin drop," J. D. said. "They were right nice to him after that."

J. D.'s wife, Ruby, had been the postmaster for twenty-one years. Now, since the place is only a branch of the post office at Gatesville, their daughter, Eula Kindler, is the clerk in charge. Eula, who had the red hair her father once had, worked from behind an ornate window in a corner of the store. She said twenty-nine families picked up their mail there and that in the old days the window in the corner served as The Grove bank.

"The funeral's at three," J. D. said. He didn't seem to be talking to anyone in particular.

"I know," Eula said. "You ought to close up about two so you can go home and change clothes."

J. D. grunted in agreement and watched his daughter. It was easy to see that she was something special in his eye.

"She's balancing the books," he confided. "It reminds me of the old postmaster and storekeeper over at Bland. The postal inspectors were always finding a difference between his books and his cash on hand, but it never rattled the old feller. 'You just check out the books,' he would say. 'If the post office drawer is short any money, I'll get it out of the store cash register. And if the post office drawer has more than it ought to, then I'll take it out and put it in the store cash register.' "

A frail old man in overalls with a frown on his face came in and sat beside the stove, which wasn't lit because of the warm

September. The porch thermometer, which had a face like a clock and "Webb Funeral Home, Gatesville" printed on it, registered ninety-three degrees.

"This is G. E. Wolff," J. D. said loudly.

Wolff looked up at him.

"He had the gin here until cotton got knocked in the head. He used to gin the dickens out of it."

"Wha'd ye say?" Wolff asked.

"I say you been ginning a long time."

"Forty-six year," Wolff said, nodding.

"He's a little hard of hearing," J. D. explained. "You have to talk up to him."

"What's that?" Mr. Wolff stirred again.

"I say you been closed a long time."

"Oh, well. Closed the gin here ten years ago. But I'm still in business in Burlington. We're partners now, me and my boy."

The two men sat mute for a while.

Finally J. D. broke the silence.

"If the old settlers could raise up and see this country, it'd scare them to death. Wouldn't know where they was."

Wolff apparently heard, because he shook his head as if in agreement.

"Remember how they used to be people come here on Saturday morning and stay till sundown? The street would be so thick with them you could hardly pass. And the dances, Lordy, every Saturday night. And the Fourth of July rodeos, they was something. Humph. It's all over now."

G. E. Wolff drove off in his pickup, and after a while A. E. Urbantke joined J. D. beside the stove. He was a tall, spare man with a weathered face. He wore overalls. J. D. said he was blind, but you couldn't tell it. He made J. D. get up and get him some Beechnut chewing tobacco and a Big Red soda pop, for which he paid cash. J. D. gives credit when it's wanted, but Urbantke has never asked for it.

After finishing his pop, Urbantke began to talk. He asked J. D. a thousand questions and answered them himself. He talked about everything but sports, religion, and politics. J. D.

never said a word, just nodded his head once in a while. Finally Urbantke left.

"Why didn't you say anything?"

"I'd be wasting my breath," J. D. said. "Urbantke wouldn't have heard a thing I was saying. He's deafer than G. E. Wolff."

Eula said Mrs. Hohle's body was already at the church, so J. D. closed the store and went home to get ready.

The next morning J. D. was open as usual at five. When the sun warmed things up, the old men began to gather on the porch as they had done the day before and the day before that and the day before on back through the years.

It was as their fathers had done, and they wore what their fathers had worn, but they did not talk as their fathers had talked.

The previous generation in The Grove had been optimistic. They spoke of the future and what a man could do in those parts with a little luck and a lot of hard work. Circumstance and events proved them wrong, but not in time to tell their sons to get out while the getting was good. So the sons sit there, old men now, and because the future holds nothing for them, they talk of the present and of holding on, and of the past.

"J. D.," one said. "Did you ever use that old gasoline pump?"

"Once in twenty-two years. I tried it the first week I bought out Gilbert. Filled it with ten gallons and sold on credit, mostly to kids. Not a one of them paid me, so I never filled it again."

They talked of the time in '27 when Clyde Barrow and Joe Hancock robbed the bank and put poor old Mr. Brown, a cripple who was cashier and the bank president, in the vault. The loot amounted to pennies, they said. And they talked of the pitiful end to which Mr. Brown came. A bank examiner found he was ten thousand dollars short, and Brown was sent off to prison and the bank was closed, never to reopen. Brown had slipped the money to his brothers, who were about to lose a land deal and needed some cash to save it. He figured to pay it back before it was discovered missing, but his brothers did not come through. The banker served his term, but died shortly after returning to The Grove. Everybody said it was from shame.

At sundown the old men went home to bed, and J. D. locked up after letting a lady put a sign in the window advertising a variety show at Comanche Gap.

Time blurred their memory. It has to be said that it was not Clyde Barrow who robbed The Grove bank with Joe Hancock, but Aubrey Ray. If Clyde was ever in The Grove, he behaved himself. The take was not pennies but $1,032. The same duo hit the bank at Copperas Cove twenty-two days later and were caught. As J. D. said, those were the days. The days of his youth.

Coryell County, 1968

Brother Nail's Magic

I mean no offense to Matthew, Mark, Luke, and John, but when I was a kid if you would have asked me who invented Jesus, I would have looked around the congregation in the Salt of the Earth Church and answered, "The women." They seemed to enjoy Him more than the men. All allusion to Jesus, in sermon or song, prayer or testimonial, brought such tears to their eyes and such exaltations, "Oh, sweet Jesus!" that I came to suspect that women, to fill this need to have some object upon which to emote, had brought forth Christ and had had Him crucified, resurrected, and sent to Heaven—the full martyrdom with a Cecil B. De Mille ending—all for a good cry.

But Brother Reid liked Jesus too, and he could make Him a living spirit that hovered over our hymning heads. On the preacher's New Testament Sundays—that is when he was in good humor—we would settle back in the hard seats with relief. His sermons took on a tone of sweetness and light and forgiveness that left us feeling a joyous content with ourselves and our little world. Brother Reid's theology was as simple as the whip and the carrot, Heaven and hell. He threatened you with one and bribed you with the other. When I was older and beginning to be bothered with questions not exactly God-fearing, I had a time of it squaring our belief in predestination with the equally strong suggestion of free will. Our elders did not beat around the bush about predetermination. We called ourselves the Salt of the Earth Church of the East Texas Primitive Baptist Association of the Absolute Predestinarian Faith and Order. In our church the rough-hewn hand of God held sway, and it was, as

preached by Brother Reid when he was irritable and reading
from the Old Testament, a stern and wrathful fist before which
we sinners trembled. Brother Reid was telling me to fight off the
temptations of the devil and be a good boy, and that if I was
successful I would go to Heaven. If I wasn't, I would go to hell.
It seemed to me the choice was mine. But then the preacher
would turn right around and say that God had foreordained
each of us to either everlasting happiness or everlasting misery.

"Granny," I asked one day as she was sending me to Cude's
for three-button snuff, "if God has already charted the course
of our lives, why should we bother about choosing between
Jesus and the devil?"

"Because he wants to test our mettle," she said.

"You mean it's like an obstacle course soldiers go through?"

"Why, I swan, Billy, that's exactly it! Yes, that's very good."

"He must be mean."

"Who, Billy?"

"God."

She looked at me, surprised. "Why do you say such a thing?"

" 'Cause it's like a torture chamber. He already knows what
He's gonna do with you, let you go or singe you into eternity.
But He puts you through it anyway, just to see you squirm and
crawl."

Granny slapped me so hard I dropped the coins for the
snuff.

But those agitating questions of honest doubt came to me
rather late, after years of blessed blind faith, years in which I
found great solace in our little country church. I remember my
conversion and baptism. An itinerant evangelist, Brother Clifford Nail, was holding a two-week revival the summer I was ten.
I had been going to Sunday school all my life, but I had not yet
been moved to make a decision for Christ. Well, Brother Nail
had the magic. He had youth and good looks and a jazzy, city
way of talking about old-time religion that was appealing to
kids. He had curly, carrot-colored hair, which he wore full like
the movie stars' hair, and a mellifluous baritone that made many
of us realize, with a self-conscious, proprietary sadness, just how
terrible was Brother Reid's twang. And, glory be to God,

Brother Nail wore shiny, pointed shoes, a bow tie, and loud, poolhall suspenders.

He was the first preacher I ever saw who got so into it that he would shed his coat in the middle of his sermon. It was the right touch. The elders did not object, not even to the well-whispered fact that what Brother Nail was taking off was not a suit coat but a sport coat.

Mother adored him. "Why, he's so natural," she sang through her nose. "Why shouldn't he take off his coat if he gets all worked up about the Lord? I think he's real cute!"

"You're right," Mrs. Cude said. "He's the new kind of preacher, just the right tonic for the young people. The Lord moves in modern ways, and those who don't see it are old sticks-in-the-mud."

Her slur was directed at poor, proper Brother Reid, who, in the brittleness of age and long habit, had not taken to the freewheeling, slangy style of the younger man. Nor did he approve. He had said as much to some of the deacons after the first few nights of the revival, but there was nothing he could do about it. In one week Brother Nail saved the souls of twenty-six sinners, better than three a night, and eighteen of them had been young people, which was considered a religious renaissance for Little Egypt. People from all over Montgomery County were filling the church each night. Even some Negroes had appeared on the scene, to hang outside, at the edge of the light, to take in this preacher everybody was talking about.

Brother Nail's line was to talk about his own sinning days in San Antonio in such a way as to make them secretly delicious and provocative to each of us. Then, when he had us hooked, he would shame and frighten us with a Technicolored telling of the ravages of those sundry vices.

After we were eaten up with syphilis and writhing and retching with the *delirium tremens*, into our parched souls galloped our Constantine, Brother Nail, to the rescue with the balm of Jesus. The choir, our Greek chorus, would break on cue into joyous, uplifting hallelujahs, and Brother Reid, from his host's chair to the left of the evangelist, would quiver like a bow and break forth thin arrows of amens, which, out of a lack of enthusiasm, fell somewhat short of the dramatic mark Brother Nail had worked so hard to hit and hold. Still, it was effective.

Brother Nail then would grow quiet, and speaking softly, almost tearfully, he would invite the sinners to come forward and take Jesus as their savior as the choir intoned:

> Just as I am, without one plea,
> But that Thy Blood was shed for me,
> And that Thou Bidd'st me come to Thee,
> Oh Lamb of God, I come! I come!

After nine nights of this, I was reduced, or lifted, if you prefer, to a state of such emotion, to the deepest dread of hell and the highest hope of Heaven, that I could not control myself. I found myself walking down the aisle, following the other sinners to redemption. It was one of the most profound experiences of my life.

After that two-week stand, Brother Nail never came to our flock again. He had come like a candy man, selling Sweet Jesus as no one else would ever do, and he took his pay—our meager offering—and left, and after a while we stopped thinking that maybe he would come back, knowing all along that he was not really one of us, that he was of other, more gossamer kind. For a time we talked about him. Another Billy Sunday in the bud. We'll be hearing more of that boy. A man who could bring sinners to the altar that way had to be destined for greater things. We remembered how gay and good-natured he had been when he came down from the pulpit and joined us in fellowship, how he seemed to enjoy the girls dropping ice cream down the neck of his shirt, how he could talk with the men and boys in a manly manner, like a coach instead of a preacher, how he charmed the ladies. And then we forgot him. The bewitcher was gone, and Brother Reid grew again as comfortable to us as he had always been.

Years later, when I was starting my first job out of college, Clifford Nail sold me a pair of nine-dollar shoes in the little Thom McAn store on St. Mary's near Broadway in San Antonio. The years had not changed him. His hair was tightly curled and seemed, if anything, more coppery than I had remembered.

He talked jive and dressed jive, down to his shiny, pointed shoes, and he sold me a pair of loafers I was not sure I wanted. As he bent over to box them, my mind went back over the years, and he was at our pulpit, taking my trembling paw to whisper his approval for my confession of sin. I stirred myself, paid him, and left, the story of our long-ago and forgotten-by-him covenant locked on my lips.

Dallas, 1974

The New Ranchers

The bison was America's only wild cattle, the only bovine animal native to these shores. They roamed the prairies in herds numbering in the millions. The plains are still worn deep where century after century they followed the same migration routes from place to place. Tom Perini can stand on his ranch at Buffalo Gap in Taylor County and show you breaks in the mountains—the Callahan Divide—where those great beasts came through regularly like furry freight trains. Their trails were so well defined that the early ranchers followed them as they herded their longhorns to market and railhead. The Dodge or Western Trail traced the trek of the buffalo.

The Indian, with his stone-age weapons and sense of conservation, could only kill the bison judiciously, when he needed meat and clothing. And he was more a maize man than a meat eater. White men arrived, but little harm was done until the human tide swept westward. Trains of emigrants lived on buffalo meat as they toiled along to the promised land. Then came the building of railways and an intensive campaign of slaughter. The noble monarchs of the plains went down before the white man's guns like ninepins before a player. With the exception of fur-bearing seals, and perhaps now the whale, no mammal of bulk has ever been slaughtered in such appalling numbers as the American bison. In part the object was food and leather and profit; in part it was sport.

The bison disappeared almost as completely as the passenger pigeon was later to do. A few, however, were left in private hands, and this kept them from extinction. The Indians had

kept a few calves as pets. They passed them to gentle white missionaries and gentlemen farmers they knew would care for them.
One of the first large-scale plantations where the bison was given
refuge was Mount Vernon, Virginia, where a man who was
destined to become the father of his country experimented in
breeding the bison to domesticated cattle. George Washington
was taking a cue from the Huguenots around Richmond, who
had been domesticating buffalo as early as 1701. These early attempts at hybridization failed, but certain cowmen continued to
toy with the possibilities.

A hundred years after Washington had befriended the buffalo, Colonel Charles Goodnight began breeding bison bulls to
polled Angus cows. This was on the JA Ranch in the Palo Duro
Canyon of the Texas Panhandle. The issue of that first cross was
always heifer calves, which, when mature, Goodnight bred back
to buffalo or domestic bulls. He called his hybrids cattalo, and
he was high on them. In the American Breeders' Association an-
nual report for 1907, Goodnight listed the "points of advantage"
which the cattalo had over common cattle. They were, he said,
immune to ticks and most diseases. They could do without
water much longer than other cattle. They were docile and easily broken and never fought. They could forage on very little.
They never drifted in storms, but stood and faced blizzards.
When they were down, they rose on their fore feet instead of
their hind feet, which enabled them to rise when weak. They
put on flesh faster than any cattle, lived longer, and produced a
steak that was lean and tender, richer than beef.

But the cattalo never caught on. Cattlemen are among the
most conservative businessmen in the world. In spite of Goodnight's stature as a rancher and breeder, they looked on his ex-
periments as fancy and frivolous, a bizarre fascination. Besides,
Bet-a-Million Gates had just introduced barbed wire to Texas,
and that was really something to hold your horses about. On the
Military Plaza in San Antonio, John Warne Gates, a Chicago
wire salesman, had thrown up a corral of barbed wire—the first
in Texas—and had challenged stockmen to pit their steers
against it. Bets were laid. The critters were penned, and the

crowd fell back to watch. The steers slashed themselves into tenderloin, but they couldn't get out. Gates collected on the wagers and won the West.

Texas was fenced in. The kind of cow that was perfect for the open range and the long drives north was no longer necessary. So the cattalo were nipped in the bud. And the longhorn, that lean old faithful forager, faded away as the favor turned toward exotic fatter stock. He, and his aboriginal predecessor, the buffalo, seemed surely to be going the way of the dinosaur. The few left were treasured like gold.

Well, gold they are—genetic gold for a new generation of cattlemen. Nine years ago some of the ranchers who still had a longhorn or two got together to figure out a way to save the breed. At that time the head count was down to about fifteen hundred, and they were scattered around the country. Today, thanks to the Texas Longhorn Breeders Association, there are ninety-eight hundred head of true longhorns, registered and regulated by five hundred breeders in America, Canada, and even a few foreign countries. The breed is growing and is being promoted and ballyhooed at shows and sales. Even the Aggies have gotten in on the act. In last April's issue of *The Ranch-man*, Dr. Stewart H. Fowler, the resident director of research at the Texas A&M Research and Extension Center in Uvalde, wrote, "Seven years of closely observing and studying Texas Longhorns have convinced me that these cattle are a genetic goldmine."

The lode the longhorn offers, Dr. Fowler said, includes genes for high fertility, easy calving, resistance to certain diseases and parasites, hardiness, longevity, and the ability to graze on marginal rangelands.

It is a shock to dig out J. Frank Dobie's classic, *The Long-horns*, and compare the pictures of the old animal with the new. The modern longhorn is massive and muscular, resembling his bony ancestor only in the spread of his horns. The difference is not blood, but skilled breeding and scientific selection. Add to that the pampering of a breed thought to be the last of its kind, from manger to lot and range, and you have an elephant with its tusks on top of its head. What bothers me about this is that

the original longhorn was not improved by man. Man ran his
ass off. The critter survived because nature's natural selection
had toughened him. He may have tasted like Aaron Simms's
Gum Cove maverick, but he kept on trucking. But Manuel
Gustamente, the executive secretary of the breeders, assured me
that the old hardiness is still there, along with a lot more meat
for the pasture.

One senses a turn in the cattle industry, away from the
grain feeding on the commercial lots and back again to grass
and grazing. Man wants his productive cultivated lands to yield
food for his belly and not for his cows. In this country we have
been feeding the grain to the cattle and then eating our hearts
out over the cost of beef. It takes about nine pounds of grain to
produce one pound of beef. Try pricing a hundred pounds of
grain, and you will understand the pinch on the cattleman. In a
land of plenty, most of his stock and standards were geared to
grain. Now he has to shift, and in the transition put beeves to
pasture that will do him the most good in the shortest possible
time. The housewife may boycott now and then, but we are,
and probably will insist on being, the world's foremost meat
eaters.

The new breeders sense all this, and none have their noses
closer to the ground swell against grain than the savvy young
operators out of Dallas who have hauled off and said, hell, let's
give the industry a dose of history and heritage along with a
splendid animal that thrives on native grass.

Super Cattle! they claim, and then go into their slogan:

The First American Exotic

The Beefalo

American Bred . . . Grass Fed

Shades of George Washington and Charles Goodnight!

They've brought the buffalo back to Texas. Or rather three-
eighths of him, and breeding down to three-sixteenths for commercial stock. The rest of the cross is Charolais and Hereford,
and so far the performance figures merit the adjectives.

This is all being played out on some of the greenest grass
and gentlest hills in Texas, the sixty-one-hundred-acre Circle K
Ranch in Kaufman County, one hour east of Dallas. The ranch

itself has been in operation since the turn of the century, give or take an owner here and an addition there. The man behind all the excitement, however, is new to Texas and ranching, a twenty-eight-year-old enterpriser from Peoria, Illinois, named Randall A. Kreiling. Randy may be a transplant, but he has taken to Texas and the play for high stakes as if he were born to the manner. He is a dashing speculator who wouldn't knock a man down who shouted "beefalo!" in a bearish beef market.

That was just about the situation Randy was in May a year ago. Backed by H. L. Hunt family connections, he had bought the Circle K the year before only to see the bottom drop out. Every cowman in American was crying. Everyone but D. C. Basolo, Jr., of Tracy, California. Basolo had leased some bison hybrids from James H. Burnett, an old-time cowman from Luther, Montana. For fifteen years Basolo had been breeding buffalo with cattle, looking for the perfect marriage of hump and rump. Now he had five thousand head of the hybrid he liked, and he was selling semen and some of the animals to anyone with gumption. One of his agents approached Kreiling. Randy talked it over with Dale Pugh, a banker buddy who had a head for cows. Dale liked the idea. He had heard about beefalo before. Dale did some homework. Randy called his brother, Tilmon, who was out at Stanford University winding up a master's in business administration and a Ph.D. in agricultural economics and computer sciences. Tilmon drove to Tracy and looked at Basolo's herd. He came back with a grin on his face and a "go" report.

The first thing Randy had to do was break the news to Joe Ellis, big Joe Boy, his general manager out at the ranch. Joe is a tried and true cowman, a sturdy veteran who puts a boot firmly down on the ground before he takes another step. He had been on the ranch thirty-seven years, since he was fifteen years old and tagging behind his father, Joe, Sr., who was then the general manager for the original owner, Angus Wynne, Sr. During the Depression old man Wynne had put together the place from a collection of worn-out farms. Joe Ellis was a fine farmer, and he and Mr. Wynne had restored the grasses and were running Angus cattle—fine cattle that won top prizes and brought top prices. Joe liked cattle, but his great love was crops, especially cotton farming, and Mr. Wynne indulged him in that. But in 1949 they lost money on the cotton, and the next year, when it came time to plant, Mr. Wynne said no, no more cotton. Convert it to grass. Well, that was too much for Joe Ellis. He quit. He quit and bought himself a farm. They made his boy the general manager.

Now here it was twenty-five years later, and Joe Boy Ellis was the compleat cow-calf man, in the way that his father was a cotton man. Joe Boy loved the land and what it could grow, but he was a cattleman first. Now here he was, fifty-two years old, listening to the new owner tell him that they had to sell the Charolais and the Brangus, that he was bringing in buffalo, or some damned freak cross called beefalo. Can you imagine what he thought?

The rumor went around that Joe Boy was going to quit, as his father had quit. Ellis says it wasn't true. "Oh," he says, "a man sometimes pops off and says things he doesn't mean." He looks away and you know it's time to drop the subject. "I'm not leaving this place unless I'm dead or fired," he adds.

By September, Dale Pugh had left the bank and joined Randy as manager of the Circle K Beefalo Management Co. Joe Ellis was still the general manager in charge of ranch operations. Pugh set up an office in Dallas preparing to promote the new breed. Tilmon Kreiling became business planner and economist. Chip Langston, a certified public accountant, joined the team. A computer system to keep track of the stock and their breeding, feeding, and performance was installed.

Joe Ellis was skeptical as hell. He had to wait and see. They decided to cool it, to keep the arrival of the beefalo a secret until they got there and proved out. The cowboys were curious. C. H. Tuttle went around shaking his head. In thirty years on the place he had never seen such goings-on.

In October they heard that Basolo had sold a beefalo bull to a Canadian for $2.5 million, the highest price ever paid for a sire. Joe Ellis still wasn't convinced. People did damn crazy things out in California.

On Thanksgiving Day the beefalo arrived from Basolo.

They'd come nineteen hundred miles in three days by truck without food or water. Sixty heifers, just weaned, and five bulls. The price tag was $72,500. Everybody on the ranch gathered around, even Gibbie Brown, the mechanic. The tailgate came down, and the heifers trotted out.

No hump. No scroungy, molting pelt. Joe had cautioned his cowboys, "You boys be careful or they'll kick your britches off." But they came down like a bunch of little Jersey heifers. Joe ran his fingers down a flank. It was pelt all right, not hair, but it was close and pretty. They had sweat glands like a Brahma, a natural air conditioning system. Each weighed about 150 pounds more than other heifers that age. He looked them over with an experienced eye, and he said, "Well, we'll have to wait and see." But he felt better.

They put them in pens for two days and watered and hayed them. Then they offered them grain. They wouldn't take it. They put them out to pasture. A bad drought was on the land. They browsed, eating briar patches and tree limbs. They weighed them every fifteen days. The gain averaged one pound a day greater than any cattle Joe had seen.

They were six months old. At eleven months they called in Ralph Shaw to inseminate the herd.

Surely the man closest to the cow of today—closer than even the bull—is Ralph Shaw. Shaw is sixty years old. He wears overalls and has never been seen on a horse. He is known in the cattle business as an AI technician and pregnancy check man. In other words, an artificial inseminator. And Shaw is in great demand because, in the words of Joe Boy Ellis, "He is the best in the business, an artist."

Ralph is a religious man. At the Circle K he was about to sock it to some cows when he looked up at Joe Ellis and asked, "Do you mind if I pray on this semen?"

"Ralph," Ellis replied, "You can spit on it like fish bait if you want to."

Ralph prayed, put on his rubber gloves, and taking advantage and aim with a little handy technology, he sent the frozen seed home. Bull's-eye!

"We had a 94 percent conception rate," Ellis was happy to report. "Fantastic!"

Those cows will calve this April. A couple of thousand three-sixteenths calves have started hitting the ground this summer on the Circle K, having been bred to commercial cows with three-eighths semen last fall. A twelve-month-old three-sixteenths beefalo bull settled thirty heifers this July. Bulls usually don't breed until they are twenty-four months old, and especially in the hottest month of all.

"We'll have to see," Joe Ellis says.

A big sign is up on Highway 243 at the entrance to the ranch. "Beefalo," it reads, "American Bred . . . Grass Fed."

Randy has put one million dollars into the beefalo.

He and Dale organized the Bison Hybrid International Association, and Dale, as president, travels around the country promoting the breed. The pitch to the cowman is that beefalo is cheaper to produce. The pitch to the housewife is that its meat is better than plain beef—more tender, with higher protein and half the fat.

Norman Fischer, a reporter for the *Wall Street Journal*, summed it up when he wrote, "It's a glamour meat, rich with history as well as flavor."

Kaufman, 1975

The Genius

The first time Lucille Williams met George W. White, she
didn't recognize him for the genius he believed himself to be.
He just looked big and busy, coming down Thomas Avenue
with his arms full of liniment bottles. His own concoction, as it
were, White's New Discovery Liniment.

His pitch was good, so she bought a bottle. It wasn't long
before he sold her himself. Now, George was no young man—
he was then fifty-eight—but he had a way about him that was
different. Even his color was a little off—kind of a gingercake.
The Mexican and Indian in him was plain to see. As Lucille
later told her mother, "He didn't look all that good, but he
seemed sincere." So they were married. Stood up before a justice
of the peace in Rockwall.

They were together for twelve years, and George White
never worked like ordinary men. He mixed his liniment in the
bathroom and peddled it door-to-door, and when he wasn't
doing that he would sit out on the front porch of their little
house over on Clyde and carve to beat the dickens. There wasn't
anything he couldn't make. He whittled a guitar and played on
it. A fiddle, too, and a mandolin. Finally, he started carving out
his life story, and Lucille could see that her man had been a lot
of places and had done a lot of things, mostly as a cowboy and
medicine man. All of it he put into his carvings, some static
and some animated by little electric motors.

George was funny about the little dolls and things he made.
He didn't like other people snooping around his handiwork.
He would work out on the front porch with a pistol in his lap.

"When I get through," he would tell Lucille, "I believe

I'll start me a road show. Get a bus, put all these carvings in it, museumlike, and travel around the country, selling my liniment as admission."

When George would finish a carving that depicted, say, a coon hunt, he would act out the voices of the hunters and the hounds and the coon. When he got it all down the way he wanted it, he would record a tape of the narrative. These recordings were to be a part of the road show.

The road show never got on the road.

But we're getting ahead of our story.

Now we must tell you that the first time Murray Smithers met George W. White, Mr. White was none too friendly. Murray, you see, is an art dealer, one who has a good eye for primitives. Well, one day Murray heard about George White's carving work from Richard Wilkinson, the guitar maker. At Murray's insistence they drove out on Clyde to see the grand old carver.

There on the porch sat White, his knife flying, a pistol in his lap, and his white beard full of chips and shavings. When Murray and Wilkinson approached, he squinted at them from under his cowboy hat and asked coldly, "Whad' ye want?"

After some fumbling around, Wilkinson got close enough for White to recognize him, and things were all right.

The old man gave them the full treatment of his art, as though he were indeed on the road and they were his audience. Murray was enchanted. The moving sculpture especially pleased him. All of it, in sum, was a panorama of the black man of the Old South and the Old West—the Negro of the clapboard cabin, of the cottonfield and watermelon patch, the takin'-in-washing-and-ironing mammy, the bronc rider and the blacksmith. Murray saw in the pieces the hand of a fine primitive artist. The meticulous detail and the fresh eye balanced against the loss of perspective and, of course, the impulse to tell a story. In every piece Murray saw a naturalness and an honesty as well as wit and irony.

He wanted to buy, right then and there, but Mr. White wasn't interested. A fellow from Walt Disney had offered him five hundred dollars a set for the moving pieces, and he had laughed in the man's face and kicked him out. White wouldn't sell a single piece for less than twenty thousand dollars. That was his price, maybe. What he wanted to do was start his own traveling road show.

Well, Murray asked meekly, would he just let Murray display the stuff in a gallery?

"Hell no," George White said, and that was it. Over the next couple of years, Murray would drop in periodically on Mr. White—once with the news that the Whitney Museum in New York was interested—but the answer was always the same.

"Nope. Gonna start me a traveling road show."

The road show never got on the road.

Mr. White got to picking at a corn on the big toe of his right foot with a carving knife and got it infected. Gangrene set in, and George White died in the VA hospital just as Lucille was expecting him to recover from the amputation.

They buried him at Bastrop, where he had been a kid.

What do you put on the headstone of a man like George White? His own assessment of himself, like the label he tacked onto his sculpture of the Jack Johnson and Jess Willard prizefight? "This event," it said, "was studied out by the greatest genius in the U.S."

"George," Lucille explained to friends, "was aware of his worth."

She finally decided on something simple. George's art would have to speak for itself. His epitaph reads:

> George W. White
> Born Sept 8, 1903
> Passed Jan 1, 1970

Dallas, 1972

Barrymore of the Courtroom

As long as we have the adversary system and as long as Percy Foreman looms up in defense of murderers, lofty thoughts of abstract justice will have to take a back seat to the blandishments of showmanship and entertainment. That is why courtroom buffs and newsmen who had reserved seats to the James Earl Ray trial go about downcast. Foreman is a spellbinder, a great lawyer and a goliath of a man with the dramatic instincts of a Barrymore. He probably acted in the best interest of Martin Luther King's killer in Memphis when he traded a guilty plea for ninety-nine years, but it was a low blow to the fans of courtroom theatrics.

After forty-four years of defending all manner of accused, Foreman's reputation has transcended the bounds of his native Texas, where, the adage goes, if you shoot someone down in cold blood at high noon, on a street crowded with witnesses, the very next thing you do is call Percy. If this smacks of overstatement, then look at the hot statistics:

In 1958 an English admirer researched the record and found that up to that time Foreman had defended 758 accused murderers. Of these, only 1 had been executed and only 52 had been sent to prison. The other 704 went free.

No one has bothered to keep an accurate count since, but Foreman himself estimates he has defended, in the past eleven years, perhaps three hundred more murder cases. Whatever the total, only one of the clients was convicted. He got a life sentence, with the possibility of a parole in seven years. So you see, Foreman improves with age. He is now sixty-five, and despite a bad back he handles something like forty criminal cases a week.

So awesome is his record, and reputation, that in a Texas House debate on the abolition of capital punishment, a legislator arose to declare, "Nobody who has the money to hire Percy Foreman has any real fear of the death penalty."

Judge Roy Hofheinz, the flamboyant owner of the Houston Astros baseball team and a longtime political enemy of Foreman, agrees.

"I don't think I'd go near him for the trial of a civil suit," says Hofheinz, "but if I knew I was guilty as hell of stealing or killing, he'd be my first choice for a lawyer."

Well, there's no question about what the outcome of such a match would be. Foreman would end up owning a baseball team as well as the lease to the Astrodome. He would love nothing better than picking Hofheinz clean with his fee.

It isn't that Percy Foreman needs the money. He entered the ranks of the millionaires more than decade ago, and he often takes cases for nothing at all. "I won't make a dime on the Ray case," he remarked not long ago. But he exacts a terrible fee on those that have more than their share, and Judge Hofheinz can be considered in such a class.

For example, one of Foreman's largest fees was the $200,000 he charged Melvin Lane Powers in that notorious Miami murder trial. Powers had no money, but his blonde aunt, Candace Mossler, who was charged with Powers in the killing of her wealthy husband, Jacques Mossler, put up $46,200 in jewelry as earnest money. Now Candy has charged Powers with assault and has filed suit contesting Foreman's fee. No one, however, doubts Foreman's ability to collect. He is so mad at Mrs. Mossler that he is suing her for $11 million.

But the biggest fee Foreman has earned to date was from Mrs. Cecil Blaffer Hudson in a divorce suit several years ago. Foreman got Mrs. Hudson custody of both of her children and a settlement of $6.5 million from the unfortunate husband.

"We're satisfied with the settlement," Foreman said after the trial. "At least it's more than Bobo (Mrs. Rockefeller) got. That is what Mrs. Hudson said she wanted—more than Bobo."

"What was your fee?" reporters asked Foreman.

"I'm quite satisfied with that too," he replied, grinning.

The Houston newspapers printed reports that his fee was a million dollars.

Because of Foreman's fame and physique (six feet, four inches, 250 pounds) and his craggy features, he is often compared to Clarence Darrow, Chicago's great criminal lawyer of the twenties and thirties. There is a strong physical resemblance between the two giants, and their methods in a courtroom are sometimes strikingly similar, but Foreman bristles at such comparisons. "I've defended more murder cases in a year than Darrow did in his whole life," he growls, and it is true. If Foreman is busier and more efficient in winning cases than was Darrow, it is also true that he lacks Darrow's intellectual profundity. If we may speak of Darrow in the present, he and Foreman are both shrewd students of human nature, but where Darrow is passionate, Foreman is persistent; where Darrow is philosophical, Foreman is practical; and where Darrow is eloquent and learned, Foreman is theatrical and tricky. Darrow always seemed to be aiming for an understanding of something larger than just the predicament of his client, while Foreman seems concerned only with the matter at hand: guilty or not guilty. One is a mechanic, and the other a poet. As Foreman snapped to a reporter after the Ray tradeout, "I don't give a damn whether there was a conspiracy; I've defended my client to the best of my ability and that's that."

But results are what counts, and no one, not even an egotist like Melvin Belli, who once described Foreman as being "a bigger horse's ass than even me," can take anything away from Percy Foreman. He is one of the great criminal lawyers of all time, as well as being an eccentric of delightful proportions.

He may be the only lawyer in the country who conducts much of his business from a bar. Now, Percy is no slob; it is a private bar, the elegant and leathery Old Capitol Club in Houston's Rice Hotel. Foreman is in and out all during the day, and no one is allowed to sit at his "desk" during his absence. When he appears at noon, the Mexican waiters pop a St. Leger Scotch and soda into one hand, without waiting for his order, and a red telephone into the other. A typed list of telephone calls, delivered by courier from his office a few blocks away, lies before him. On this particular day there were twenty-eight calls. He answers them all while chewing a bloody filet mignon and conducting interviews with potential clients—three women who sit sipping drinks at the next table. The three ladies want divorces, and they patiently await their turn with the great defender. "Why shouldn't they be patient?" Foreman cracks, "I'm buying their drinks."

The ladies are intrigued at Percy's telephone conversation; they gaze at him with such envy that you know they are comparing him with the crummy husbands they want to shed.

His voice is deep and male, sometimes scratchy, sometimes resonant:

"Now, listen, sweetheart, I don't want to hear about your hospital experience; what's your legal problem . . . ?"

"Honey, if I owned the courthouse, and a lot of people think I do, I'd send you justice in a sealed envelope. . . ."

"He's an honest man, but like a lot of honest men he stayed honest for lack of temptation. . . ."

"No, honey, I don't pretend to be the greatest lawyer who ever lived or even the greatest living lawyer, but on the other hand I don't deny it. . . ."

And so it goes. He walks from the club to the courthouse to his office with a retinue of clients and admirers. On this day it is more like a circus scene out of Fellini. There are some thirty women with him. They are all in debt to him now because he has just gotten them off the hook of a very disagreeable charge: lesbianism. They had all been arrested in a notorious bar, and the police said every one of them was wearing slacks. Percy had paraded a group of fashion experts before the jury and had won hands down. "Hell," he commented with grand amusement, "it's perfectly acceptable, fashionable even, for ladies to be seen in public places with pants on."

It is to be a busy day. He gets a postponement on a narcotics case, helps a Las Vegas client negotiate a profitable contract with the Howard Hughes interests, confers with the sister of a woman in prison about getting the sentence reduced, discusses litigation with some theater people. Then there are the fifty murder cases in various stages of preparation, forty divorce suits, and he doesn't know how many other assorted criminal matters hanging fire.

His office is a godawful eyesore. On the facade facing the street a two-story-high goddess of Justice, executed in a gold mosaic, stands above the Golden Rule written in tile over the door.

"I was completely tight when I agreed to that," he says sheepishly. "I may have to change it to the goddess of Liberty. My clients don't want justice, they want liberty."

His office is a huge, dark, rather chilly cavern. There are no decorative appointments: a plain hard bench, a few straight-backed chairs, a desk for his lone secretary, a cluttered little cubbyhole in the corner for himself.

"Disorganization," he bellows, "is the keynote of this office."

His desk looks like a candidate for a bonfire. It is laden with piles of papers and briefs, books, a bowl of stale walnuts, a pot of phony flowers, a pair of tiny red leather boots (perhaps for his daughter), a Marlin 30-30 carbine (security for a fee in a divorce case) and a clutter of strong-smelling pipes. Foreman is so casual with his bookkeeping that he often lets checks from his clients stack up for weeks on his desk before he opens them and signs them for deposit in the bank. Not long ago he opened a pile of dusty mail and found in one of the envelopes a client's check for twenty-seven thousand dollars. The date on it was a year old. "That," says Percy, "was my largest temporary oversight."

Yet he will haggle over the smallest fee. Once he talked a pathologist client out of his microscope and a musician out of her harpsichord. He will accept anything in lieu of a cash fee.

That is why he owns dozens of little houses and lots all over Texas, two and one-half pounds of diamonds, and storage sheds around Houston packed with stoves and refrigerators, furniture and antiques, and God knows what else. He even accepts cars as fees, which is why he now has about thirty automobiles sitting in garages about town. Rather than paying a storage fee, he allows the garage owners to strip the cars for parts. The result is that most of the cars are not in running condition and really are not worth more than junk. "I just don't have time to mess with all that stuff and practice law too," he says. "Maybe if I retire, I'll get time to look after it all."

Prosecutors and peace officers pray every day for Percy's retirement. The story that shows how lacerating he can be for the defense happened in 1950. Foreman, in defending a Mexican accused of murder, so maddened Harris County Sheriff Buster Kern and Texas Ranger Captain Johnny Klevenhagen that when the jury foreman said "not guilty," Kern and Klevenhagen, normally two taciturn, rock-faced men, emitted cries of rage, leaped the courtroom railing, pounced on Percy, and proceeded to pummel him until they were restrained.

"See," one juror exclaimed triumphantly to another, "I told you the sheriff did it."

As usual, Percy had tried the officers in defense of his client.

His technique is nearly always the same in each case he defends. First, he is always prepared. "He is a very thorough lawyer," says William Walsh, a former partner (Percy and his partners never last long together). "He knows what the evidence will be."

The second thing he does is go for a jury trial (the Ray case was a rare exception), because, as he point outs, "I'm pretty good with juries." He never picks people to serve on juries who work as scientists or accountants. "I want people who work with other people and know human frailty," he says, "I like social workers and teachers and bartenders to be on my juries."

And once the trial is under way, Foreman tries his damndest to keep the attention off his client. "You should never allow the defendant to be tried," he says, "Try someone else—the husband, the lover, the police, or, if the case has social implications, society in general."

Percy Foreman, damn him, was born in a log cabin in the piney woods of East Texas. His daddy was a sheriff, and Percy picked up his love of the law through hanging around the local courthouse. He dropped out of high school but finally worked his way through the University of Texas law school. Even then he had the midas touch. He managed to save sixty-seven thousand dollars while a law student. "How did you do that?" someone once asked him, and he replied, "I sold cars, worked as a booking agent for the Marine band and made speeches as a Chautauqua lecturer."

Of this initial capital he blew eighteen thousand dollars on a terrible binge in Chicago in 1927.

"I decided I had better get back home before they took it all," he said. "So I went back to Houston and put the rest into my law office. That was the beginning."

It's just as well that Percy left Chicago. Clarence Darrow was still practicing there with eleven good years left in him. Comparisons would have been inevitable, invidious as they are. Yet the years have humored Foreman. "Hell," he growls, "Darrow and I are both interested in the same things, the rights of the poor and oppressed. If they're not poor when I meet 'em they are when I'm through with them!"

Houston, 1969

Don Pedrito

Consuelo sweated, and Raúl cursed the heat with his thoughts. If he had not been a loyal son, Raúl would have cursed his mother. Such stubbornness! He had tried to persuade her not to make the pilgrimage to Don Pedrito's grave in the heat of the Texas summer. Wait until October, he had said.

"Mama, it's just logical to wait. Then Aunt Lupe can drive you down and I won't have to skip two days of classes."

"Mi hijo, I must go on the anniversary," she had replied. "I made a vow in the name of God, and in the name of Don Pedrito. I know it will be hot and a lot of trouble for you, but you are the only one to take me. I do it for you. You should be grateful."

"Mama, I don't mind the trouble. It's you I'm concerned about. It will take us half a day to drive to Falfurrias. You know that. It will be hard enough on you in the heat driving down, but the walk from town to the grave—Por Dios, it's four miles— will kill you. Think of your heart."

But nothing he could say would deter her. If he would not drive her, she would ride a bus. She had made a vow in the name of God and in the name of Don Pedrito.

Consuelo had started the trip in the back seat of the hot little Ford, but she had gotten carsick. Now she sat beside Raúl, the taste of vomit and its humiliation in her mouth and beads of sweat on her lip.

Raúl looked at her. How squat and pitifully uncomfortable she seemed, all corseted and draped in black. Yet so stolid in her sense of mission! She caught his gaze and forced a self-conscious smile. A sudden tenderness for her moved within him, and he patted her plump knee. Of all of us, he thought, perhaps because of her naïvety, she is the strongest. The car rolled around a bend and into the Falfurrias city limits.

They stopped at a café to rest and refresh themselves, and then Raúl drove through town and out onto the Riviera highway. At the city limit sign he stopped the car, and Consuelo got out, draped a black shawl over her head, and started walking east on the shoulder of the road.

He battled with himself, offered a prayer for her safety, and slumped into the seat to wait.

He would move the car often enough to keep her within sight. He looked at his watch. It was past noon. If nothing happens, he reasoned, she'll be there in three hours. The sun burned down, boiling the tar in the asphalt road. As the black figure of his mother grew smaller, Raúl realized what he had to do. He drove up beside her.

"Wait," he said. "I'm going to walk with you. There's a gas station back up the road. I'll get somebody to drop me off here and leave the car at the cemetery."

And they walked together to the tomb of Don Pedrito, fulfilling a vow Consuelo had made shortly after the birth of Raúl twenty-one years before.

Her first two sons had died in infancy, and Consuelo, at her mother's instruction, had taken a photograph of her new baby and left it on Don Pedrito's grave with a prayer and a promise. If Raúl lived to manhood, she would, in the name of God and Don Pedrito, walk the miles from town to the grave on her son's twenty-first birthday.

Consuelo is dead now, and Raúl likes to tell his children the story. He is an educated man who is skeptical of the old superstitions, but he tells it with a gentle tolerance, and with just enough "ooh" to make you wonder.

Don Pedrito is still the most popular *curandero* in Texas, though he has been dead for fifty-eight years. His followers come from throughout the Southwest, even from Mexico, to pay homage to his memory and to ask for guidance. On All Saints Day they camp around his tomb by the hundreds. The Catholic

Church has not officially recognized his saintliness, but they who believe in him say it is only a matter of red tape and time. He was, no doubt, an unusual man.

His name was Pedro Jaramillo, and he was born in Guadalajara, Jalisco, Mexico, sometime around 1827. The story goes that Jaramillo, while working as a shepherd for half a bushel of corn and five dollars a month, suffered an affliction of the nose. The pain was so great that God spoke to him. Jaramillo was instructed to bury his face in the cool mud of a river bank for three days. He did so and was cured, though the malady left his nose warped like a pig's snout. The voice then instructed Jaramillo to cure his ailing master, which he did by prescribing the first thing that came to his mind.

This is how they say Jaramillo became a faith healer. No one knows why he came to Texas. Some say he was charged with being a *brujo*, a sorcerer, and that he fled for fear of imprisonment.

At any rate, one day in 1881 Juan Berrara, a Falfurrias rancher, noticed Jaramillo in a band of whiskey peddlers he met on a country road. Jaramillo was a strange-looking little man. He was dressed in a rude, black suit. His flat face was of a yellow cast, his beard was long and grayish, and his sombrero was as broad as an umbrella.

"Who are you?" Berrera asked, struck by something odd in the little wayfarer.

"I am Don Pedrito, a *curandero* by the grace of God," Jaramillo replied. Ah, the beauty of their language. It even has a quaint quality when translated, "I am Little Peter, Esquire, a healer by the grace of God."

At Berrera's invitation, Don Pedrito built a *jacal*, a wigwam, on Los Olmos Creek and began practicing what appears to have been a curious concoction of folk medicine, benevolent witchcraft, and common-sense psychiatry.

At the time, there was only one doctor (at San Diego) between Corpus Christi and Laredo, and Don Pedrito's brand of medicine was highly popular. He claimed no healing powers for himself, and he was always careful to say, "In the name of God," before prescribing remedies. He used herbs and waters and fruits and leaned heavily on the patient's respect for the super-natural. He was brutal with skeptics and was supposed to be able to spot one instantly.

Chat Vela, a horse trader, was such a skeptic. "If that old *brujo* cures me," he sarcastically told friends, "I'll give him ten dollars and a fine pair of gloves." Then he rode to Los Olmos, where Don Pedrito put a poultice on his sore leg. Vela gave the old healer a bunch of gourds and started to leave the tent.

"Aren't you forgetting something?" Don Pedrito asked.

"Do I owe something more?"

"You should say, 'Here old *brujo*, is ten dollars and a fine pair of gloves.'"

Don Pedrito was only mocking the horse trader. He never, it is said, asked for money for his services, but accepted whatever else was offered. He knew better than to take money. Once during a visit to San Antonio the crowds that greeted him were so large that police had to be called out. They tried to jail him as a medical quack, but he was freed because he had not charged for his consultations.

When a group of gringos talked of stopping Don Pedrito's practice, the San Diego physician, Dr. J. S. Strickland, warned them: "Don't. How do I know that Don Pedrito's prayers do not do more good than my pills?"

And when Lafayette Wright, an altar boy, made light of the old *curandero*, Father Peter Bard, the parish priest, re-proached the youngster. The priest and the old wizard were friends. The bell atop the church in Falfurrias was a gift, worth fifteen hundred dollars, from Don Pedrito.

Don Pedrito had become a man of substance. Don Antonio Hinojosa made him a present of one hundred acres of land, which was cleared for farming. During the drouth at the turn of the century, Don Pedrito was said to have fed the poor in the northern half of the county from his delta crops.

His camp on the creek grew in proportion to his fame. He still saw patients in the little tent, but other dwellings and tables were added to take care of the constant flow of people. On week-ends, hundreds waited in wagons to see the *curandero*. Don Pe-drito hired women to cook for the crowd.

When the railroad came to Falfurrias in 1903, the postal service picked up, and Don Pedrito found his table stacked with hundreds of letters, all asking for cures by return mail. The poor man could not read or write. He had to employ his adopted son, Serviano Barrera, as a secretary. He had raised Serviano from boyhood and had made him go to college. They would sit up late into the night answering the letters by the light of a lantern. The patients would enclose postage stamps as payment, and Don Pedrito would stuff them into a barrel. When the post office in San Antonio ran short of stamps, an inspector was sent to Los Olmos to get some from Don Pedrito. He found nine hundred dollars' worth in the barrel. He found three five-hundred-gallon barrels of unopened letters. Don Pedrito and Serviano simply couldn't get to them all.

Because of the letters, many of Don Pedrito's prescriptions have been recorded for posterity.

To a Señor Feliciano he wrote through Serviano, "Bathe seven nights, at whatever hour you choose, entirely nude, soaping yourself in cold water; have no guard."

When a doctor couldn't get a grass burr out of a man's throat, Don Pedrito suggested, "Drink salt water, all you can stand." Of course the man vomited up the burr.

Don Pedrito cured Antonio de la Fuerta, a vaquero on the ranch of J. Frank Dobie's father, of asthma. A woman who had migraine headaches was told to have her head cut off. She exploded into violent anger at the prescription. But when she cooled down her headache was gone.

Mrs. William Sutherland, wife of the postmaster at Paisano, also had severe headaches, but Don Pedrito said he couldn't help her. "You have no faith," he told her. But he cured Mrs. Sutherland's daughter, Mabel, of a toothache, it was said, by making her wear a roasted clove of garlic in her shoe.

One day a group of vaqueros brought a man on a stretcher. For some unknown reason, they complained, he was unable to walk. His legs looked sturdy.

"Throw him into the creek," Don Pedrito instructed.

They threw him in and stood on the bank and watched. The poor man managed to crawl out alligator fashion.

"Throw him back," Don Pedrito said.

They threw him back. He managed to stagger out. The therapy was repeated all afternoon, and by the time it was over the poor man was kicking and running like a mustang.

Don Pedrito fell sick on July 2, 1907, and refused medical attention. "If God is ready to take me, I will go," he told Serviano.

He died the next day, but not before telling Serviano: "I will try to return to you. After three days, unearth my coffin."

Serviano didn't have the nerve to do it. But he visited the grave every day until he died in 1959 at the age of seventy-two.

Serviano once told his daughter, Mrs. Horacio Villarreal of Falfurrias, "He was a good man, Don Pedrito, but very strange, sometimes frightening. He would dance at midnight in the brush."

Several years ago a wealthy Tejano gentleman from San Antonio had a small, hutlike shrine built over Don Pedrito's grave. The inside is never without light, for the faithful keep hundreds of votive candles burning.

It is an eerie experience to sit alone at night in that hot little temple, four miles from town on a lonely ranch road, and wonder who put a woman's tresses in the pickle jar placed on the concrete tomb, or who hung a baby's shirt and trousers on the wall and why, and who comes to collect the coins left at the altar and why.

Falfurrias, 1965

The Outcasts of
Western Heights Cemetery

"Morris Kermit Woods, I'll never understand you," Sarah said wearily. "All that fool scribbling! Every night! Such a waste!" She let the dog in and went muttering to bed.

He had not heard her, not really. In most things they were compatible, but in this he had to go it alone. He had learned, when he sat down to put his thoughts on paper, to shut her off somewhere between the ear and the brain. She had never read anything he had written. This hurt him, for the writing had become the most important thing in his life. He thought up the stories during the day as he drove about Dallas in his taxicab. It didn't hamper his driving. He found he could make right turns and small talk with his passengers and still keep the flow of the story moving through his mind. Sometimes he would try one out on the more gregarious passengers. When the reception was good he could hardly wait to get home and put it all down.

Morris lived in a rented cottage on Neal Street in the Oak Cliff part of Dallas. Now, way past supper, he sat at the kitchen table under a dim light, his pipe and tin of Prince Albert and his pads of ruled paper all in place, and he wrote slowly, laboriously, his thick fingers curled around a stubby pencil.

Once a flower happened to grow in the midst of a weed garden and a weed growing nearby betrayed the blossom to the weedmaster as he came strolling through his garden, saying, "Look Master, a despised flower dares to grow among us and spoil the conformity of the garden . . ."

Morris chuckled, pleased with himself.

. . . betrayed the blossom . . .

It had a nice ring. He licked the lead in the pencil and pressed it to paper.

. . . so pluck it out from us. . . .

Morris Woods was a fat man, Falstaffian in appearance if not in manner. The front of his shirt and the lap of his pants were pocked with holes burned by cinders from his ever-smoldering pipe. He was fifty-eight years old. Darken the hair, remove the jowls and replace the missing molars, deflate the bulb on the nose, and speculate how handsome Morris might have been forty years ago in the hills of Arkansas. A flower in a weed garden? Well, not then, not a 1932 school dropout.

The lack of a formal education, the want of the rote of reading, writing, and 'rithmetic hurt him now. He had never learned to spell very well. The mind forms thoughts with words, and Morris had the words. He had them, for he had listened well. They just came out a little warped on paper, phonetic little cripples. But for a long time, for most of his life, as a matter of fact, this was not to bother him.

He was too busy working at this and that, busy raising a family, busy with the agony of divorce, and busy courting Sarah out of loneliness. He had found her in Arkansas, sacrificing her youth and middle age to take care of her old daddy and mother.

And then, when he was fifty-seven, Morris changed. It came at him all of a sudden, it seemed, from inside. Something seemed to break loose in his brain—not his sanity, not that, for his perception was heightened. It was kind of an explosion that shook away the rust in his head. The wheels of his mind ran out of the ruts, and he began to think about things that were, to him at least, wildly intoxicating. Sarah, who worked every day sorting clothes at Mercury Cleaners, said it was foolish fancy. She didn't read him, but he talked all the time.

Once a truthteller was born into a world of liars . . .

"Morris? Come to bed."

One night you rise up screaming in bed and your daddy comes and takes you near the fire.

"What in the world is the matter? What has frightened you this way?"

"I don't want to die."

After a year of night-writing, Morris had finished, to his satisfaction, nine stories. He stacked them neatly in a box labeled "The Complete Works of Morris Kermit Woods" and took them to a public stenographer.

"Lady, how much would you charge me to type this stuff out in manuscript form?"

She sifted the pages.

"Fifty dollars."

Ummm . . . that was a chunk. Boy! Was it worth it? What did the lady think? Did she figure he could do anything with the stories if she did 'em up nice?

"I think so," she said, taking his fifty dollars.

Morris made the rounds with his manuscript. He left his stories with professors who had ridden in his cab. He left them with people who passed themselves off as literary agents. He mailed them to publishers. No one encouraged him. All rejected his offerings, and some did not bother to return them. Yet Morris continued to write nights and persevere by day.

All of this I came to know about Morris after his soiled and rather sad-looking manuscript found its way into my hands one evening last summer. Morris and I struck up an acquaintance in, of all places, an old graveyard. I was down in the weeds and neglect of the Western Heights Cemetery, up on the Trinity bluffs along Fort Worth Avenue, trying to find tombstones of some Oak Cliff pioneers, when I looked up to see Morris bearing down on me like some sinister sexton.

"If you're looking for what I think you're looking for," he declared, "then you're way off the mark."

"Oh," I said, brushing the stickers off my pants leg, "You mean the Coombeses?"

"No," he said, "I mean Clyde Barrow. Isn't that who you're looking for?"

"Clyde Barrow the outlaw?"

"Yep."

"Well, no, not really. The Coombes family is supposed to be out here. . . ."

"No markers like that," Morris said emphatically. "I've read 'em all many times." He looked at me steadily. "Most people," he went on, "come out here to see Clyde's grave."

It was odd the way he put it, as if to challenge me for being indifferent to such an attraction. *Everyone* came to see Clyde's resting place. It was *the* thing to do, almost an affront to *be* there and *not* do it. Not wishing in any way to slight Barrow's memory (or, for that matter, Morris's seemingly sure guardianship of it), I quickly explained that I had come into the cemetery ignorant of Mr. Barrow's presence there, but that now that I was apprised of it, wild horses and rolling stones could not keep me away. Morris lost no time in taking me to it.

The remains of Clyde Chesnut Barrow lay in a small family plot fenced with rusting pipe. Clyde was buried beside his brother Buck. They shared a common headstone which said they were gone but not forgotten. Certainly it was true in Clyde's case. Buck had died in bed in July of 1933, when he was twenty-eight. Clyde had died in a hail of bullets from the guns of lawmen. This, of course, was in 1934 when he was twenty-five.

"Where's Bonnie?"

"Well," Morris said, squinting and squatting at the foot of the grave, "she wanted to be buried here with Clyde, but her family put her in Fishtrap. Fishtrap is an old cemetery over north of Singleton Boulevard. But Bonnie's not in Fishtrap no more. In the forties they moved her to Crown Hill out on Webbs Chapel Road."

Clyde's gravelly grave was not neglected like most of the others in the cemetery. His and those of his family were swept up in clean little mounds, and someone had left a jar of plastic flowers at the foot of Clyde's.

"I buy 'em and put 'em there now and then," Morris said. "They fade or the kids steal 'em."

"Are you related?" I asked, nodding toward the dead under discussion.

"Naw," he said, "I'm just a cab driver. Now there's Barrows left, because I see them come here. They take care of the graves, too. You see, I live a few blocks away, and I like to come up here and sit, so to speak, with the dead." Morris looked at me keenly.

"It sounds funny, I know, but how I explain it to the wife is that this cemetery does for me what church does for her. If you know what I mean?" He looked so earnest that I was drawn to this big, rough spirit.

We fell into a deep conversation there among the crab apple trees and tombs. Below us, to the east of the Trinity, the skyline shimmered in the heat like a mirage. Hours passed. The sun sank behind us, mellowing like a benign eye, and cast an orange spell upon the heights. We filtered the dying light like lenses, and felt in our lungs the noxious vapors that rose above the roar of the homeward-bound traffic. The skyline glowed.

"My throat's dry," Morris said at last, and we retreated to Luchia's Psychic World Nite Club, where we quenched our thirst and where Morris laid upon me his benediction, his complete works. He had run home to fetch them. Now he sat expectantly as my eye fell upon the first page.

"I can't read them with you staring at me," I said. "Give me a few days and I'll get back to you."

He was up and gone. Usually I hate to read manuscripts that are foisted upon me by strangers, but Morris was clearly and resolutely his own man. What was it he had said in the cemetery? Something to the effect that the dead were outcasts, especially an outlaw like Clyde Barrow, and that he, Morris K. Woods, being an outcast himself (if self-styled), was naturally drawn to them. Hell, I understood that and hoped Morris was another Bret Harte.

He was not.

But had Morris read Nathanael West or Lewis Carroll or Dr. Seuss? Had he heard Charlie Mingus? Had he been on the road with Kerouac, to the opera with Barth, or simply writing in watermelon sugar with Brautigan? Morris had peopled his stories with prophets and tramps and comics. Their adventures were zany, right out of a Three Stooges comedy, but there was also a serious undertone in the pieces.

The influence of the Bible was obvious, and Morris certainly seemed to have the countryman's basic distrust of preachers. All his prophets were false ones.

There was a short fable on truth, a fable on a prophet, who, like Jonah, finds himself in the belly of a whale. Morris had his Jonah exit the whale by means other than the mouth. Aha! N. West's anal fixation.

There was a skit about a man and a woman dueling with riveting guns, a piece on a satyrlike preacher walking on Turtle Creek, a wildly disjointed bit about a man who preferred to sleep with pigs because his wife snored in stereo.

The most sustained piece—it ran thirty-nine typewritten pages—was about the adventures of Hum de Drum (obviously Morris) and a cross-eyed prophet called the Rigidly Upright Most Rightly.

Mr. Most Rightly was the founder of the Revised and Modernized Version of the Ancient Totem Pole Faith, forerunner and ancestor of all religions. Hum de Drum and Mr. Most Rightly go forth into the land of the Mighty Ma Ha in search of "Sampson's scalp and the source of his strength." They came upon Creosote Joe, a talking crosstie in a railroad trestle. They pluck him from his prison and take him along, singing:

> *Fakes, phonies, defrauders are we*
> *Boom, Boom de Boom*
> *We rob the stupid and poor, do you see*
> *Boom, Boom de Boom*
> *Religiously Uprighted, most Rightlys are we*
> *Boom, Boom de Boom*

They find "Sampson's" scalp and use its powers to cow the Mighty Ma Ha's army. Creosote Joe, who claims to be a totem god, is returned to his place in the trestle. Hum de Drum says to Mr. Most Rightly:

You must know very well that there is no God either totem or otherwise embedded in among the splinters of wood inside Joe's creosote overcoat and if we would chop him open, we would see nothing inside but splinters. Now isn't this the real honest to God truth?

Yes, what you say is true.

We met at Luchia's. We had a few beers.

"Morris," I said at last, "Your pieces are interesting and original, but they're not stories yet. They are wildly bizarre snatches of fables and such, but you haven't developed them."

He seemed crushed. We had a few more beers.

"Don't be discouraged," I said. "A lot of writers start with less than you show here. You've got great ideas. You handle dialogue well, and there's a nice Biblical roll to your sentences. But your stories have no structure that I can see."

He shrugged. "Hung up and haywire, huh?"

"You can get off and going," I insisted. "Look, in anything you undertake there are certain rules and techniques you have to learn and abide by, at least until you've proven you're good enough to break the little rules in order to set higher ones. You've just hauled off and started writing, and there's a lot of needless trial and error between what you want to say and what you actually say. Go to the library and get a book or two on how to write a short story. The professors who write these things are usually dull with no gifts, but at least they can teach you mechanics. And for God's sake get a dictionary. I don't mind the misspelling, but no editor will take you seriously when you make simple grammatical mistakes. And don't call your manuscript 'The Complete Works,' because it isn't. You're alive and still writing."

Morris sighed. "I can't go back to school at my age," he complained.

"I don't mean that." We had a few more beers.

Before we split, I handed him my copy of the summer, 1968, issue of the *Paris Review*. "Read the interview with Jack Kerouac," I said, "that ought to inspire you."

He grabbed me by the arm. "I need something now," he said, slurring his words. "You're blowing the whistle on me. I've stopped and you've got my attention. But I'm dumb. I don't know what I've done wrong, exactly. Well, write me a ticket, paint me a picture."

"Okay," I said, not so steady myself, but heady enough to pick up on his play. "If I were Police Chief Don Byrd, I'd give you a ticket for driving without brakes. If I were Lamar Hunt, I'd kick you off the tour for playing tennis without a net. And if

I were Werner Von Braun and you were an astronaut, I'd say you were stabbing at the stars with a toothpick."

Luchia shooed us out.

I saw Morris one more time.

We met at the Athens Strip and watched Diana King. Morris was sober in spite of the beers. He didn't say much, just stared at Diana. "Me and my old lady, we split," he said at one point.

"Where'd Sarah go?"

"She got a room over at the Last Frontier Motel. Hangs out at the Lone Star Christian Singles."

"What is that?"

Morris laughed bitterly. "What it sounds like, where the drys and the devout hang out."

He handed me the *Paris Review*. "Kerouac's a good man," he said.

"You should read him."

"I've started *On the Road*."

"Did you get some books on style and technique?"

"Yeah," he said, "but I took 'em back." He leaned across the table and bit down on his pipe. "Look," he said, "I know you were trying to help me, but I don't see no sense in doing what the book says. If a man wants to write like ever'body else, well all right. But it's not for me. I don't like to think of my mind as a tow-rope. I don't follow nobody."

But of course that was not true, not even of Morris K. Woods.

It was not long after that I got a letter from Morris. Just a note really, written from the Greyhound Bus Station. Sarah had found her another man, a Mexican who painted on black velvet, and they had run off to Houston. As for Morris, well, he was running off, too, heading to Lowell, Massachusetts, where if the stars were right, he intended to meet up with and make a friend of Jack Kerouac. Kerouac was his kind of man, a wild man, a master of outlaws, and surely he could teach Morris a thing or two.

Poor Morris, I thought. He doesn't know he's following a dead man.

Kerouac had croaked years before.

Dallas, 1975

On the Banks with Larry Bowman

Long ago, before Gutenberg, Marconi, Edison, De Forest, and the like, it must have been easier for ordinary people to live lives of quiet obscurity. Of course they had their heroes and villains, the famous and infamous who shaped their times and found a place in history. But the men and women who stood out from the rest were not omnipresent as they are today. The great marched through history, but not through millions of living room television sets. While Caesar fought and Christ died, the mass of humankind went on about its business, ultimately affected, of course, but uncomprehending. Even in a gossipy, with-it Paris, how many of his subjects would have recognized Louis XIV on the street? Men were known by their deeds, not their image, and it took time for the word to travel. It may seem odd to us now, but in those days the news followed events instead of the other way around. Thus, it was quite natural for common people far from the maddening crowd to fill their days with the mundane and never ask why.

Historian Will Durant was once challenged to sum up civilization in half an hour. He did it in less than a minute, this way: "Civilization is a stream with banks. The stream is sometimes filled with blood from people killing, stealing, shouting and doing the things historians usually record, while on the banks, unnoticed, people build homes, make love, raise children, sing songs, write poetry and even whittle statues. The story of civilization is the story of what happened on the banks."

Today, however, our banks are run over with the commotion from the stream. We are inundated with instant history. And if not that—the real thing—we get what passes for it: pseudoevents acted out by simulated heroes. If it gets on our nerves and is unsettling at times, it is also strangely compelling. We want to jump in, too, and make our mark, if only for a moment. Make an appearance. Grab a headline. Receive some notice beyond the boundaries of the wife, the boss, and the boys at the bowling alley.

Why not? After all's said and done, most of us come down to a few dreary lines of agate in the classified death notices. What sorry summings up they are of human lives. I read a decent one last summer from the *Saint Louis Post Dispatch*, and it is worth passing on:

> Noel Digby died Sunday, June 15, 1975, of cancer at the age of 50 at his home in Kirkwood. He left behind him a good wife, 9 children, 3 grandchildren, a mother, 2 sisters, a brother and a big adopted priest, a nice but leaky house, a lot of love and a lot of things he still wanted to do. He was at peace with himself and his God. In his words, while he wasn't as perfect as he wanted to be, he was "the best damn Noel Digby there ever was."

Beautiful. I'm certain, though, that Noel Digby would have preferred the cash to the credit, that he would have opted for a little press before rather than after. If that's all that is being handed out. Happily, it isn't. The media are loosening up, giving more fanfare for the common man. It isn't out of heart, really. The common man is a customer, a consumer with money now and interests that go beyond the daily grind of nine to five. In his leisure he is a market and a taste to be catered to, and television is his medium. It is the great common denominator. It reflects him in its ratings and programming and appeals to him in its advertising. And more and more it offers him the spotlight and the microphone.

Never have ordinary people had such entrée to the stream and stage of life. We have left the banks of Durant to become transfixed with McLuhan's message. We watch it like Baptists at the river, with total immersion. And daily we see people like ourselves sprinkling themselves in its benediction, being baptized to broadcasting as members of the cast.

Only the self-important and the demented think they have

to run for something or try to kill the president to get on TV. The rest of us realize all you have to do is register for some game show or call a press conference. The real Rose Renfro ran for council, but there are millions of Roses out there who would settle for a shot at "Let's Make a Deal" or "The Price is Right" —thus the plethora of game shows which mix celebrities and common folk in some kind of inane guesswork. It is a sure-fire draw for the audience as well as the contestants. What the Roses are assured of is that they will rub shoulders with some Hollywood square while being seen by millions of other ladies from the Kroger Price Patrol. And don't think the ladies at home behind the picture windows are not rooting for the Rose on the tube. For the moment, there on the screen with the boy from "Bonanza," rolling the dice or whatever for a cruise to the Caribbean and a wardrobe of doubleknit, she embodies the possible dream.

Larry Bowman is a young man who has spent his twenty-six years on Will Durant's bank, which in this case is the working man's suburb of Carrollton. Larry didn't build his home, but he is paying for it. He and his wife Janet make love and raise children, and while they don't sing songs all that much or write poetry or whittle statues, they keep busy and try to stay ahead of the bills. Larry is a mail carrier out of the Carrollton post office. He has a pretty good deal, he figures, because he gets to deliver half his route in a jeep instead of on foot. The Bowmans have two daughters: Deanna, five, and Tuesday, who was born on a Friday a year and a half ago. They have their heads set on having two more, they hope boys.

Postmen are not paid handsomely, so Larry is taking accounting at nights at Richland College. He hopes to do a little moonlighting as a tax man. Because of these pressures, Janet allows Larry a night or two with the boys. He plays penny-ante poker with his friends now and then, but the big night is Thursday, when he bowls at Hart Alley in the citywide post office league. His teammates are the boys from the Carrollton P.O.: Donny Beckham, Chuck Haynes, Larry McDaniels, Eugene Martinez, and sometimes Johnny White. They've been together two years and call themselves the "Far Outs." Last year Larry bowled a 163 average, which placed him at the top of the team. This year his average has dropped 15 points. Larry says it is because they have slicked down the lanes at Hart. His buddies tease him and say it is because he got the big head from being on television twice in three days.

Back in August, WFAA-TV (channel 8) launched a locally produced show called "Bowling for Dollars," with sportscaster Verne Lundquist as host. The idea was bought from Plaster Television Production in Towson, Maryland. The format proved irresistible. Every night from 6:30 to 7:00, Monday through Friday, seven people from the heartland hereabout come out of the audience at Forum Lanes in Grand Prairie to talk with affable Verne and try their hand at bowling for dollars. Each contestant gets two balls. If they get two strikes they take the jackpot. Missing that, they get fifteen dollars for one strike or a dollar for every pin that falls. Each bowler must share his winnings with a pen pal who is watching at home, which builds up the interest at both ends. The bowlers rarely hit two strikes in a row, so the jackpot often builds to several hundred dollars over a period of shows.

The productions are taped in advance every Tuesday out at Forum. The crew sets up at 6:00 A.M. The contestants and their families and friends gather at 9:00, and Verne Lundquist comes on at 10:00 to start the first show rolling. They tape until dark, until five or six half-hour shows are in the can. By the time it is over Lundquist is as weary as a Dallas Cowboy after four quarters with the Pittsburgh Steelers. He has jawed on camera with thirty-five or forty-two folks, prying from their modest mouths a little patter about their work and hobbies and families. It is stock stuff, as banal and trite as the circumstance dictates, and yet somehow it is often touching and revealing. The people, if a little awkward, are not embarrassed. Hell, they are excited and expectant. They ask to be on. They send in cards and hold their fingers and watch faithfully and wait, hoping to be selected. So do the pen pals.

Lundquist, as always, comes across as a good guy. It is a herd to handle in one day—a week of air time—but he gets through it. He makes no pretense about it. It is money and exposure. It is not as lowbrow as a night at the wrestling matches, but it ain't the thirty minutes of news it replaced. Lundquist had doubts about doing it. There was some bitterness among his fellow journalists when the station cut the evening news hour by half. But an hour of unrelieved news speaking was drawing only 54,000 viewers. "Bowling for Dollars" has built the audience in that time slot to 80,000. In the ratings it still falls behind "Adam 12" on channel 11 and the nationally syndicated game shows on channel 5, but it has taken up considerable slack. And more than 250,000 people have sent in cards asking to be a bowler or a pen pal.

This is where Larry Bowman, our Carrollton postman, came in. He filled out five cards and mailed them in September. The Plaster Television computer in Maryland scans the stuff and selects contestants to fit a system calculated to let the jackpot perk, but not too long. Things like bowling average, age, occupation, and sex are food for thought for the computer. Anyway, early in December it spewed out Larry's name, and eight days before Christmas he found himself at the Forum, shaking Verne Lundquist's hand and talking about being a postman and telling how, on Christmas Eve, he was going to dress as Santa and deliver candy to all the three hundred households on his route. "Great, fantastic, and who did you bring with you tonight?" Verne asked, and Larry had Janet stand up along with the girls and his brother Rickey and Janet's older sister Imogene so the camera could catch them. Larry also said hello to his sister Julie and her husband Gale, as well as his other sister Mary Theresa and his parents and Janet's parents. He was not through. He had to say hello to all the people at the Carrollton P.O. and the same to all the bowlers down at the Hart Alley post office league.

He reached into a pot and drew the name of his pen pal, which Verne announced as Mrs. L. R. Gustafson, of 5215 Landino in Fort Worth. She would share half of anything Larry won.

Damned if he didn't get up there and roll two strikes.

The jackpot was the highest it had ever been: $2,540.

His pen pal, Marie Gustafson, did not jump up and hit her head on the ceiling of her living room. Remember, the shows are taped. She knew nothing. She would have to wait until the show was aired on the night of December 26.

Christmas Eve came, and that day a channel 8 crew filmed Larry making his rounds as Santa, delivering candy instead of mail. He watched himself on the night's news.

The evening after Christmas, more fans than the Cotton Bowl can hold watched Larry hit the jackpot bowling for dollars on channel 8.

In Fort Worth, Marie Gustafson jumped out of her chair.

When the check for $1,270 arrived in the mail, she put a little in savings and spent the rest renovating her kitchen.

Larry Bowman spent all his paying off a loan company debt. Janet said all she got of it was a glance as he signed it away. No matter, Larry says, it was the coolest thing that had ever happened to him, next, of course to marrying Janet. Now strangers at the bowling alley recognize him. The *Postal Journal* of Branch 132 featured Larry in a page-one story along with two pictures—one of him and Verne shaking hands and the other of Larry in his Santa suit. He also got a mention in the *Bowling News*. One thing puzzles him, though. He never got so much as a thank you from Mrs. Gustafson.

Dallas, 1976

The Sanctified Lady

"I never did get in love with men people," the Sanctified Lady said. "I was born lovin' the Lord, not worldly things. I tried a man once, when I was sixteen, but after a year I went home to Mama. It jus' wasn't for me."

"Too young, perhaps," the visitor ventured.

"No," she said, "I was speakin' in tongues when I was twelve. My ways were set."

"Why do you think you are sanctified?"

"Because the spirit comes on me."

"What happens?"

"I tremble and shake and talk in tongues, and the Lord gives me something about you, and I get to lookin' real hard at you."

"What do you see?"

"The future. I prophesy."

"Do it to me."

"I'm not in the spirit. It comes on me when the Lord wants it to, not when I want it. Sometimes it's a burden and I kind of dread it."

"Why?"

"Well, it's bothersome. I was a cook for a Smoke-a-Chick stand for five years, and the man finally got tired of me scarin' the customers and fired me. I'd get in the spirit when I was waitin' on people. It jus' didn't work out.

"I been put out of a lot of churches because I'm a prophet. Like when I was goin' to the Fifth Ward Church. I'd see the death of certain members comin' and I'd pin black crepe to their seats. Sure enough, they'd die. Everybody got mad at me, but it wasn't my fault."

"Maybe not, but I can see how people would avoid you."

A smile darted across her broad, black face, and she took off the black cloche that hugged her head.

"Many people come to me for help," she said. "A man came this morning with a heart spell. I laid hands on him and he sighed and was all right."

"Do you charge for this?"

"Whatever they want to pay. The Lord provides for me and my children."

"You have children?"

"I raise other people's children. They leave them here like stray cats."

A small girl came in crying.

"What's the matter, child?"

"James hit me."

"Tell him to come here. Just a minute."

She wiped the kid's nose with her skirt tail, kissed the round little cheek, and sent her out again.

"That was Shirley," she said. "Shirley's five. Her mother left her here four years ago and never came back. Then I've got Oscar, Dollie Mae, Gloria, James, Berta, and Pat."

She parted a curtain and pointed to a roomful of sleeping infants. "Now these tiny ones ain't mine to keep. I'm jus' baby-sittin' for their mothers. I got six now."

James, a lad of eight, came in yelling, "Mother, Shirley hit me first."

"Oh, James," she said wearily, "All you'll come in now. Time for dinner. We got grits."

"Thought you didn't like worldly things?" the visitor said assuringly.

"Huh?"

"The kids. Flesh and blood."

"No," she replied with a broad smile, "Don't you know angels when you see them?"

Houston, 1964

The Ghost of Amon Carter

Oh, East is East, and West is West,
And never the twain shall meet. . . .
Rudyard Kipling

Fort Worth is where the West begins.
Dallas is where the East peters out.
Will Rogers

. . . If I want to get something done in Fort Worth,
if I want to get some of these people up off their
asses, all I do is remind them, 'You don't want
those Dallas bastards to get ahead of you.'
Amon G. Carter

If Dallas and Fort Worth have a problem, it's
primarily Fort Worth that has a problem.
Al Altwegg, *Dallas Morning News*

Now that is the way it was with Dallas and Fort Worth from
the very beginning—a kind of hyperbolic squaring off, in strong
language and deed, of two very different peoples and places.

The thirty-three miles that separated us were, in John
Gunther's words, "a chasm practically as definitive as the Continental Divide."

One senses it still, even in the obvious way the country
changes. Dallas is softer, shady, an edge of East Texas. Fort
Worth has a bigger sky, is a little hotter in the summer, colder in
the winter, drier, and higher—the West. We are city; they are
country. Visitors like them better. We try too hard.

Oh sure, there have been, over the years, perhaps half a
dozen attempts to ameliorate the differences. Some of them, especially the most recent, seemed about to succeed. The demog-

raphers in Washington have already begun thinking of us as one standard metropolitan area. And for a while it looked as if the Dallas–Fort Worth Regional Airport and Tommy Vandergriff's amusement park would tame the no-man's land between us.

But thank the devil and all that is divisive, the ghost of Amon G. Carter has come back to haunt us. The ancient antagonism of arch-rivals yet lives. It rises, like a phoenix, on the wings of that upstart airline, Southwest, which insists on flying out of a field Fort Worth is loath to love. Ah, the rich, recovered acrimony of it all. Kipling and Carter are vindicated. We have resurrected, for a brief moment, an old hostility that was probably more humorous than it was harmful. Indeed, it was often helpful. Don't you realize the rest of the country turned to see us, in our boisterous difference, and put us on the map as neighboring opposites, freaks on the forks of a river? We used to be something to see, along with the six-legged calf in Daisetta and old John Nance Garner in Uvalde. We attracted not only attention and passers-by. The competition was keen, generating tandem explosions of community and commerce on the Trinity that now threaten, in a telling twist of fate, to annihilate those very individual identities which propelled us into such sharp profile. Where once we had two distinct cities, we now have a hyphen which, spoonlike, steadily and surely stirs us into a homogeneous blend.

That blending is inevitable, of course—a process of expansion and integration that all great urban regions experience, especially in America, where growth is unchecked and ungoverned. We have married in our mass Dallas and Fort Worth and have brought forth a ranking as the tenth largest standard metropolitan statistical area in the United States. The day is not far off, the experts tell us, when Dallas–Fort Worth–Denton will be one strip city, perhaps with metropolitan government. Whether this will be for better or for worse is difficult to say. Certainly it will be, bombs to the contrary, and people have a way of living with whatever the times dictate. But what have we lost?

One cannot help pausing in the midst of all this urban transmogrification to look back, like Lot's wife, at the two sep-

arate cities that once thrived on the plains *plainly apart.* If salty
individualism is a sin, they were the Sodom and Gomorrah of the
Southwest, their towers of babel beacons of boosterism and self-
promotion. Then the impulses were just as venal as they are
today, only vertical instead of horizontal. A city was more spiral-
ing than sprawling in its run for the money.

No individual stood taller in either town than Amon Carter.
He ruled Fort Worth like a feudal king and tormented Dallas
like an elusive and legendary bandit. There was a joke that
went:

> What is the fastest thing on two wheels?
> Amon Carter riding through Dallas on a bicycle.

Carter's great weapon, of course, was the *Fort Worth Star-
Telegram.* He was the publisher, and he wore it on his hip like
a six-gun. For every shot he fired into the air in celebration of
Fort Worth and the West, he matched it with a well-aimed snipe
at the spreading and in comparison effete rear end of the cos-
mopolis east of the Trinity. Ouch! In spite of its dignity, Dallas
had to grab ass and duck for cover. The man was a barbarian.
And indeed, Carter looked and played the part. He was Indian
big and sodbuster boisterous, a rough who had come off the
prairie to out-moxie and outmaneuver Fort Worth's toughest
characters. When he was alone with home folks, Carter could
be quiet and as conservatively dressed as a Dallas banker. It was
when Easterners came to visit, or when he went East, that Carter
threw on his cowboy hat and spurs and sidearm. And hell, East
to him was Dallas and anything beyond.

In 1928 Carter was in Houston as a delegate to the Democratic National Convention which nominated Al Smith. An elevator operator in the Rice Hotel kept ignoring his signals from
the sixth floor, so Carter, to the astonishment of his companion,
a newspaperman from Baltimore named H. L. Mencken, pulled
his Sheriff's Special and fired several shots into the elevator door.
After that the Rice Hotel elevators ran like Mussolini's trains,
especially when Amon G. Carter was registered.

He saw himself as a western Robin Hood, stealing from
rich Dallas to give to poor Fort Worth. In the days of the Old

West, Eastern gentlemen were often bushwhacked on the trail and relieved of their valuables by bandits. Well, Amon Carter was a one-man gang against Dallas for nearly thirty years. It was true that the real West was dying, even in Fort Worth, but Carter carried it on, in costume and corporate deed and derring-do, right on up through the 1930's. In 1934, when Carter had American Airlines move from Dallas to Fort Worth, the *Dallas Journal* cried, "We have once more been Amon Cartered!"

But Carter rode alone.

He was one man in Fort Worth against a thousand in Dallas.

Fort Worth was way behind when he took up the fight, and it was still trailing when he died. Not in terms of dignity of life or graciousness. It seems, in many ways, to be a better place in which to live than Dallas. We're talking about the Brownie points chambers of commerce get for bigness and all that come-on about market potential. But by God, Carter gave it all he had. "That man," Vice-President John Nance Garner once remarked, "wants the whole government of the United States to be run for the exclusive benefit of Fort Worth, and if possible, for the detriment of Dallas."

Carter was by far the most vivid of the feuders, but he was not the first. Historian A. C. Greene insists, with a smile, that the rivalry between Fort Worth and Dallas began before there was a fort and before Dallas had a population of one. In the spring of 1842, John Neely Bryan, the founder of Dallas, rode west thirty miles to Bird's Fort and asked the two families there to come join him on the bluff above the Trinity. The two family heads, Captain Mabel Gilbert and John Beeman, did not hesitate in accepting Bryan's offer. They had ventured a bit too far for comfort. The year before, they had turned their faces toward the grand plains, which they could make out at sunset through the traceries of the twigs and leaves of the southern forests. It beckoned to them in a way we can only imagine. They were woodsmen and farmers. All their lives they had hacked their hearts out clearing patches for farming. Before them lay land that was rich and rolling. It stretched to the horizon, and there was hardly a tree on it. God had done their work for them. Indians be damned! But now, after only a short time, they were eager to return to the company of another white man and to the sanctuary of cover. The place known as the beginning of the West would have to wait a few years before another outpost was established.

Major Ripley Arnold came along in 1849 to establish Camp Worth on a bluff overlooking the Clear Fork of the Trinity. Press Farmer opened a store in a tent. The Fort Worth to Yuma, Arizona, stage line was established. The fort folded after four years when Arnold was killed in a duel with another officer, but the settlement was secure, and Fort Worth was on its way, in a modest manner of speaking.

So, of course, was Dallas. John Neely Bryan was a shrewd town promoter. He had publicized Dallas widely and had the jump on Fort Worth. Even before Camp Worth was established, Dallas could boast that it was a county seat with a post office and a newspaper. Already Dallas was looking to the North and East, and certainly to the Deep South, for the exchange of goods and services and people. Fort Worth looked to the West. It was a natural inclination. Cowtown became Cowtown because it was the last stop before Kansas and the first one on the return trail, a handy oasis for man and beast. Saloons, hotels, whore houses and stockyards sprang up as the cattle drives came through.

As early as 1871, Captain K. M. Van Zandt, a lawyer-banker, had been trying to get rail service for Fort Worth. But Dallas again got off to a head start when in July, 1872, the Houston & Texas Central puffed into the new depot just east of the courthouse. Old John Neely Bryan was there to greet the locomotive, chewing on a hunk of barbecued buffalo with an ear cocked for the oratory of John Henry Brown. By the following year, the Texas and Pacific, which was being built from Marshall, Texas, to San Diego, California, had committed itself to reaching Fort Worth. But the panic of that year stalled the march of the railway just as it neared Dallas. Dallas was able to bring the H & TC on into a depot six blocks from the courthouse. Fort Worth fumed and faded. Even the cattle drives had dropped off. It was about that time that a Dallas editor wrote that Fort Worth was so quiet a panther had been found asleep on Main Street. This seemed to arouse Cowtowners. They set out with picks and shovels to finish the laying of the rails. They reached Fort Worth in July, 1876. "At last," wrote Buckley B. Paddock, editor of the *Fort Worth Democrat,* "we hear the shrill scream within the corporate limits, arousing the panther from its lair!"

For a time the panther was to vie with the steer as a symbol of Fort Worth. Baseball teams and dance halls bore the name. It was Paddock's genius that turned a slur into a brag. He was, even more than Van Zandt, the Amon Carter of his generation. Once, when Paddock learned that some big eastern financiers were headed for Dallas to have a look around, he got on the train in Texarkana and made their acquaintance. He passed out special copies of the *Democrat* which extolled the virtues of Fort Worth. By the time the train rolled into Dallas, all the easterners could talk about was Fort Worth. An official reception was scheduled for the next morning. When the Dallas mayor arrived, he learned that Paddock had hired all the livery rigs in Dallas and had taken the visitors to Fort Worth.

It was nip and tuck. Dallas opened its state fair in 1886, so Fort Worth answered with its first fat stock show and rodeo.

Every day Paddock ran a map on the masthead of the *Democrat* which showed nine railroads branching out of Fort Worth. Eventually it came true, and Paddock built one of them. He served as mayor eight years, until the turn of the century.

By that time both towns had established themselves. The competition turned, briefly, into cooperation. The Northern Texas Traction opened an interurban service between Dallas and Fort Worth that lasted for thirty-three years. Fort Worth was the gateway to the West, and out there money was being made in oil as well as cattle. Oilfield supply houses and petroleum companies moved in beside the stockyards and meat packing plants. Fort Worth, smaller than Dallas, was a loose-gaited, working man's town. Dallas was derisive. "News has reached here," one editor wrote, "that two men have drowned in bathtubs in the last six months. It proves that Fort Worth has at least two bathtubs."

But Fort Worth was appealing, especially to real easterners

who were bored by the affectations of Dallas. It was on the edge of the frontier, big enough to be comfortable and white-man safe, but close enough to the wide open spaces to be exciting. There was a string of saloons and whore houses just north of the present convention center called Hell's Half Acre. Butch Cassidy hid out there. Quanah Parker, the chief of the Comanches, made Fort Worth his home off the reservation, and Teddy Roosevelt came to ride and hunt.

This side of the Trinity we had become a cosmopolitan little city, already the world's largest inland cotton market, smugly claiming more banks and better hotels and restaurants, more parks and amenities than any other place in the Southwest. The first skyscrapers began to sprout.

Even the federal pork that was beginning to be ladled out to the states seemed to suit the individual tastes of the river rivals. If Dallas got the Federal Reserve Bank, then Fort Worth had to have Camp Bowie in World War I. From then on Fort Worth, befitting its name, would be armed to the teeth, first with soldiers and then with the hardware of war it manufactured. Dallas, of course, grew more and more into an abstraction, a paper money and credit town. But we must not forget that when Fort Worth got Camp Bowie, Dallas also got the aviation center which eventually would spark the bitterest row between the cities: Love Field.

The war was over in Europe, but a civil war cloud was rising over the Trinity like a frown. The man who would fan the flames was finding a voice on the *Fort Worth Star*. Amon G. Carter started as an ad salesman. Within a year he and the editor, Colonel Louis Wortham, had squeezed out the investors. They merged with the *Telegram* to become, in 1923, the largest newspaper in the South. From then on Carter lived but for one thing: the glorification of Fort Worth and West Texas. Houston had Jesse Jones, and Dallas had Robert L. Thornton, but not even those giants could claim the power over their cities that Carter commanded over his Cowtown. Dallas had many strong men, several almost equal in power to Uncle Bob. If Fort Worth had any, they became weak in the face of Carter. He wanted everything his way, and he got it. As a kid he had run away from home and school by the time he was eleven. As an old man he told *Time* magazine that he had read only fourteen books in his whole life. He made millions, but cared little about money. He had given most of it away by the time he died. Yet in his prime he made the earth shake and lesser men quake.

In 1929 Borger was a boom town crazed by oil fever. Within months an estimated forty-five thousand men and women had encamped there to strike it rich, one way or the other. The situation got out of hand, and Governor Ross Sterling sent in the state militia to enforce order. When Carter heard of it, he stormed into the *Star-Telegram* newsroom and shouted to an editor, "Get me Sterling." When the governor answered the phone, Carter spat into it: "Sterling, you goddamn son-of-a-bitching idiot!" and went on to dress down the governor for giving West Texas a bad name.

In 1933 Carter sat in Harry Sinclair's New York office. Behind Sinclair's desk was a map of the Sinclair Oil Company offices around the country. Carter noticed a red pin stuck in Dallas.

"Harry," Carter asked, "Does that mean you've bought out Pierce [Oil Company] in Dallas?"

Sinclair nodded yes.

Carter got up and walked to the map. He pulled the red pin out of Dallas and stuck it in Fort Worth.

Harry Sinclair laughed.

But he moved the office to Fort Worth.

In 1934 Carter and Fort Worth suffered what seemed to be a setback. Dallas was chosen as the site of the official Texas centennial, after some adroit moves by R. L. Thornton, Fred Florence, Harry Olmsted, Arthur Kramer, and A. Maceo Smith. It was not to take place for two years, however, so Carter got to work on his side of the river and created a competing attraction, the Texas Frontier Centennial, which opened in 1936 at the same time as the official version across the river. At the entrance to the Dallas fair Carter had created the world's second largest sign (the largest was a chewing gum ad in Times Square), which read: "Forty-five minutes West to Whoopee. Dallas for education. Fort Worth for fun." And it was fun. Billy Rose, hired at one thousand dollars a day, staged a fabulous review called "Casa Mañana" on the world's largest revolving stage. Among the attractions was fan dancer Sally Rand. Dallas drew the most visitors, but Fort Worth's effort was popular and the most publicized, mainly because Carter brought in one thousand newspaper columnists from around the country. Damon Runyon quipped, "In Dallas the women wear high heels. In Fort Worth the men do."

Amon Carter seemed superhuman. During World War II his son, Amon, Jr., was captured by the Germans and sent to a prison camp in Poland. The authorities lost track of him. During the liberation the old man flew to Europe and, with the help of correspondents, found his son and was reunited. On the way home Carter stopped off in Italy, climbed to Mussolini's balcony, and shouted, "Hooray, for Fort Worth and West Texas!"

Carter did not always win. He could have had Magnolia and the Flying Red Horse atop the Fort Worth skyline, but he blew it.

Texas Christian University lost more football games to Southern Methodist University than it won.

And Carter himself remained a provincial, outsized as he was. His fanaticism for Fort Worth was so strong it blinded him to larger opportunities. He could have been secretary of state under Franklin Delano Roosevelt, but he turned it down. Eventually his chauvinism came to sound silly.

"I have not been accused of being partial to North East Texas and Dallas," he said, "and I don't believe you have to live in Fort Worth and West Texas to get to heaven—although it wouldn't be detrimental, in case you get an invite."

And sad.

An exaggerated story, which is still at large, had it that Carter always took a sack lunch when he visited Dallas rather than begrime his stomach with rival victuals. He had done it only once, really, but the story became a symbol of Carter. In later years many people in Fort Worth grew weary of the caricature. A Fort Worth chamber of commerce official dared to tell an audience of Dallas business leaders, " I think it would be ridiculous if anyone brought a sack lunch to Dallas."

Carter exploded. "By God," he wrote, "I speak for Fort Worth! What hurts me is that one thousand of Dallas' leading citizens think someone else is speaking for Fort Worth."

He was old then, in his seventies, and more and more he was challenged. A young politician named Jim Wright got away with it handsomely, deeply humiliating Carter. Wright announced for Congress without going to Carter for approval and support. Carter cursed him out in a page-one editorial. Wright replied in kind with a thousand-dollar ad in Carter's paper. "The people," Wright wrote, "are tired of 'One-Man Rule. . . .' You have at last met a man, Mr. Carter, who is not afraid of you . . . who will not bow his knee to you and come running like a simpering pup at your beck and call."

That was in 1954. Wright won the election. Within a year Amon Carter was dead. Wright, of course, still serves in Congress, and the *Star-Telegram* is now solidly in his corner.

Amon Carter did not live to see the D-FW Turnpike opened in 1957. Or the historic joint issue of the *Dallas Times Herald* and the *Star-Telegram* in 1960, promoting the Trinity River canalization. Or the forming of the North Central Texas Council of governments to share in government grants. What could he have said about the latter-day Fort Worth mayor who confessed to being "in a sort of love affair with Dallas"?

Carter was vigorous up to the end, so he did not groom anyone to take his place. He was incapable of that. And no one took his place. Not really.

"The problem is that none of us have any harness marks on us," one of his friends observed after his death. "Amon did all the pulling."

There was, indeed, a dearth after his death.

Even five years after, one economist, commenting on the stagnation of Fort Worth, declared that it was "reaping the harvest of dictatorship."

But then Fort Worth perked up. The 1960's saw downtown Fort Worth revitalizing itself around a striking new convention center. The restoration continues with the new water garden. New leaders are emerging. They are less flamboyant and certainly less authoritarian, but they work well together within a broader spectrum of the community. Certainly they believe in détente with Dallas. The regional airport is the crowning jewel of that mutual statecraft. It is a fact, the magnet around which the two communities will touch until one is indistinguishable from the other. East and West will meet, and Kipling and Carter will be as quaint as once they were apt.

Southwest Airlines will only be a little flap in the breeze of an inevitable assimiliation. And because Fort Worth is the smaller and the more anachronistic (which in this case is a compliment as well as a condemnation), she will more readily lose her present identity in the mass.

Perhaps it is just as well that Amon Carter died when he did, never suspecting such outrageous reaching across the Trinty. He died with his boots on, as they say in the West, right up to his big ears in battle.

Dallas–Fort Worth, 1976

Ravel's Elegy and the
Sad Violinist

Every evening, after the sun had spent its fire and was failing in the funereal sky, the old man would emerge from a little house in the southwest part of Houston and walk solemnly around his dying garden, playing a violin.

He was a small man, with a Basque face set on a neck as slender as a girl's.

He always played the same melancholy little piece on the violin.

I saw him many times as I passed in those days. He never deviated; once around the weedy garden slowly, stroking the fiddle that sang one sad song.

Sometimes a black cat followed him.

I spoke to him in greeting once. Surely he must have heard me. But he went on as if in a trance, a shocking sadness in his face.

The neighbors knew little about him; that he lived alone with a menagerie of cats, talking to them as though they were people. He kept to himself.

I moved from the neighborhood and forgot the strange little man.

Then one day, years later, I was listening to a recording by the Orchestra du Theatre National de L'Opera, Paris.

Memories of the strange little man came flooding back.

It was the same tender elegy he had played evening after evening in his garden.

Ravel had written the little rondo in 1899 and had named it "Pavane pour une Infante Defunte," or "Pavane for a Dead Princess."

The composer wrote that he had composed the pavane as an elegy "for any dead child."

I learned that Ravel had lived alone with a family of Siamese cats and that he talked to them as though they were children.

Ricardo Vines, an old friend of the composer, once described him thus:

"A delicate, Basque face, with a clear profile, raising from a slender neck and narrow shoulders. . . ."

With a dozen questions burning in my brain, I returned to the old neighborhood in search of my strange little man.

The little house, the dead garden, were gone, replaced by the gleaming columns and spans of a freeway.

No one knew where he had gone.

Houston, 1960

The Cowboy

Decatur sits on seven hills just east of the Trinity River's west fork and just north of where the West begins, right on the divide which separates the Grand Prairie from the Western Cross Timbers. No matter from what direction you approach, the same three landmarks catch your eye and beckon: the eighty-year-old Wise County courthouse, the eighty-four-year-old Decatur Baptist College, and the ninety-two-year-old Waggoner mansion. Each is a splendid memorial to Victorian pomposity, Texas turn-of-the-century style. They are unnecessarily massive —the courthouse is equally rococo—and so out of character with yesterday's horse and cowboy and today's pickup truck culture that you wonder about the builders and what they had in mind.

Well, what they had in mind were some rather lofty notions about man and his place in the universe. Man was at the center of the cosmos, answerable only to himself and God. Over at the Baptist college, Brother J. Lawrence Ward taught that life was a grave moral responsibility, a stern judgment which only the pious and the elect survived unto Kingdom Come. Out on the Waggoner ranches the test of life was just as strenuous in a quest for earthly rewards. By that time the primal age of technology was in full steam, even in Texas, and men with motors and gas lights and the telegraph felt themselves in full conquest of their hours on earth. Certainly Dan Waggoner was, and all he had was a slave boy and the spit in his hands. He fought off Indians and hard times—or rather, they tried to fight off him and the hard time he gave them. At any rate Waggoner won the day, turning a scraggly herd of longhorns into sixty thousand head that ranged over seven counties and one-half million acres. He made himself a baron, and so he built a baronial mansion to match his deeds.

Of all the fabulous cattle empires in Texas, only three ever surpassed the Waggoners' in sheer size: the 3-million-acre XIT Ranch in the Panhandle, the 1.8-million-acre Matador Land and Cattle Company just below the Panhandle, and the 1-million-acre King Ranch on the southern coast. The Chicago corporation which owned the XIT disbanded it in 1912, and the Scottish syndicate which ran the Matador had sold it off in parcels by 1951. In 1954 ranch historian J. W. Williams wrote that "if the great ranches are to be weighed according to value, the vast oil wealth of the owners of the Waggoner Estate might tip the scales in their favor."

The oil, however, came years after Dan Waggoner's death in 1904. They discovered it in 1903 while drilling water wells. They considered it a damn nuisance. Dan's son, W. T., is said to have abandoned the wells in disgust, plugging them with fence posts. "Damn it," he bellowed, "cattle can't drink that stuff." Tom, as they called him, had better things to think about. He was once heard to say, "A man who doesn't admire a good steer, a good horse, and a pretty woman—well, something is wrong with that man's head."

Tom was a chip off the old block, not one of those sons who is repelled by his father's epic appetite. At the age of eighteen he had herded up the Chisholm Trail with the old man. Their bond was so close that he and the widowed Dan married sisters. The mansion in Decatur was imposing but not removed from the workaday ranch life. It was headquarters and hotel for the hands as well as residence for the Waggoners. Eventually their operation outgrew the environs.

They bought one-half million acres in Vernon. When the old man died, he left Tom an estate valued at seven million dollars. Thirty years later when Tom died, he left his two sons and daughter an empire worth seven million dollars multiplied a hundred times over. It included cattle, oil, banks, buildings in cities, and a famous race track and horse breeding farm called Arlington Downs—now the site of Six Flags over Texas and home of the Texas Rangers baseball team.

Today there are no males left to continue the estate in the Waggoner name. Electra Waggoner II, the great-granddaughter of Dan, survives in Vernon as Mrs. Johnny Biggs. Her husband managed the estate and the ranch until his death in August.

The heritage, if not the inheritance, has been taken up again in Decatur by an unlikely young man who until a year ago was a stockbroker, first in New York and then in Dallas.

John Waggoner is the first male Waggoner in sixty-five years to live in Wise County. And the folks around, still steeped in the Waggoner saga, assume he is back with old money to burn. John is quick to point out that he is "one of the poorer relations."

He likes to recall that his great-granduncle Dan came into the county with 242 head of cattle, six horses, and a slave. "What do I have?" he asks, and replies, "Sixty steers, my wife, Betsy, and my boy and girl—none of which are inclined to kowtow to me."

John also has a promising business, the Ford tractor dealership, which he bought ten months ago. But that is not why he came to Decatur. Rather, that was the how, the practical opportunity he hit upon to carry out a dream that came to him five years ago when he had just about had it with the city.

"I'll admit what I'm doing," he says. "I'm playing play like. Play like I'm a cowboy. And I'm in dead earnest about it. I want to have the best herd of whiteface Herefords you've ever laid eyes on. I want to stand in the middle of my land and not see the end of it. Maybe I won't make anything big like that. The time of the full enchilada is probably passed, but I can raise my family on the land and ranch and farm and feel like a man instead of a mouse in a rat race. Hell, after all, I'm a Waggoner, and that counts in this county. Maybe that has something to do with it. I know it's the reason I'm here instead of someplace else."

The road to John Waggoner's house curves in front of the

Dan Waggoner mansion. Every day he passes that way. You know he can't help but play like about it, too. Certainly movie-goers have, ever since its replica was center stage in the movie *Giant*. Another family lives there now, so John can only day-dream. "You know," he laughs, "I had at least three girls back home in Wichita Falls tell me they would marry me if we could live in that house."

His grandfather, Jeff Waggoner, had hauled the stone in wagons from Fort Worth to build the mansion. Jeff was eighteen at the time, a cowboy for Dan and Tom. His father, John Thomas, was Dan's brother and had married a sister of Dan's first wife. So Jeff was a double first cousin to Tom. When Jeff married in 1888, five years after the mansion was completed, he and his bride spent their honeymoon night in one of the bedrooms. It was a good start. They had seven children, and Jeff didn't do badly for a poor relation. He and his brother, John, bought a section of land from Dan Waggoner and established themselves as ranchers in their own right. By the time Jeff died in 1943, he had left his heirs several thousand acres with oil wells on them. His second son, T. J., Jr., our John's father, became the executor of the estate, settling in Wichita Falls to look after the family oil interests.

John had been a three-year-old, bouncing on his grand-father's knee, when the old man was seized with a stroke that proved fatal. That became important to John as he grew; it made him feel closer to the departed old cowboy than he otherwise might have. His uncle Merle, his father's older brother, then became the rancher in the family, and John loved to listen to Merle tell stories about grandfather and the cowboy days. It seemed to him, a kid growing up on a tame, tree-shaded street in the better part of town, that life in the old West was infinitely richer. Funny, daring, dangerous—all the things boy swash-bucklers play at.

Like grandfather's name. He had been christened James Monroe, after the fifth president, but then his father changed his mind and renamed him Jefferson Davis, after the Confederate president. That was fine until his father came home from the Civil War complaining that "every nigger and mule on the road" was named Jefferson Davis. So the boy became Thomas Jefferson—T. J., or simply Jeff.

Jeff Waggoner had made the last great roundup, the "Centennial Hunt," in the spring of 1881. The next spring he had ridden the last big trail drive the Waggoners would make from Texas to Kansas, just a few months before the Ft. Worth–Denver Railroad reached Wichita Falls. He had ridden with Indian scouts; he had roped with Gus Pickett, who in 1902 bested Will Rogers for the world's champion steer roping title; he had shared a bunk one night with Jesse James; he had even, years later, had a Cadillac stolen by Bonnie and Clyde.

All these stories John took to heart; he could hear them over and over again. But the most stirring vision he cherished of his grandfather was a rather quiet one. He could see the old cowboy camped on a great plain, darkness surrounding him, with nothing but a small campfire to illuminate his circumstance.

But that was long ago. The campfires were out now. The cowboys had come into town to put their sons through college. John's father had gone to Southern Methodist University. John himself was encouraged to do the same and take up a suitable profession. And he did that with varying degrees of success and failure. As a broker in New York he had made some big deals and had had some bad luck. He had come back to Texas to try to put together something in Dallas. It fizzled. He joined first this firm and then that. John could not stay put. Something kept pulling at him.

One Sunday afternoon, five years ago, John and Betsy and the kids passed through Decatur on the way to Dallas from Wichita Falls. All of a sudden he said to Betsy, "Let's go see Crystelle!"

Crystelle Waggoner was a cousin of John's father. She had never married. She lived alone on the Ditto Nine, a ranch she had inherited from her father, John, the brother who had gone in with Jeff Waggoner. The ranch ran for several miles behind the old Waggoner mansion. Jeff had sold out to his brother, and in 1936 John had built a rambling headquarters house on the place. He had died in the house. As a kid, the current John Waggoner had spent weekends there, running up and down the creeks with his brothers playing cowboys and Indians. When he and Betsy and the children stopped at Crystelle's place, down the road a piece from the headquarters house, it was the first time in years that John had seen his second cousin. She had never met Betsy and the brood.

The visit was brief but enriching. John's children took to Crystelle and the outdoors as he had when he had been a boy. Crystelle wasn't doing much with the ranch. Once she had raised race horses, but now she was taking it easy. She had rented out the headquarters house. John and Betsy were enchanted by it. It sat at the end of the road like a fine old boat tied to the end of a long pier, and all around as far as the eye could see was an ocean of rolling prairie. Crystelle seemed amused at their enthusiasm. She had never liked the place. It was too big for one woman, and she was tired of fooling with it and tenants.

A week later John was sitting in his office in Dallas when he got a letter from Crystelle Waggoner.

"John," it began, "I'm making you a gift of the house in Decatur."

She went on to explain that she was doing it because she liked them and their yearning for the country and because it was partial payment for all the kindness and consideration John's father had showed her over the years.

That was the turning point in John Waggoner's life. At last, at thirty, he knew what he really wanted to do.

Every weekend, he and the family lit out for Decatur, which is fifty miles northwest of Dallas. "It didn't make a damn if it was New Year's Eve and party time or if our best friends were in town," John recalls. "We couldn't wait to get out here."

For five years he saved his money and waited for a business opportunity to open so they could make it in the small town. That opportunity came in October, 1974, when Roy Eaton, a Dallas television personality, tipped off John that the Ford tractor dealership was up for grabs in Decatur.

His old stockbroker buddies wouldn't know John Waggoner now. He goes to work in a straw hat with dung on his boots. It is crap, but it is pungent with promise. John's steers and calves have won prizes at shows in Fort Worth. They graze on land owned by Cousin Crystelle. And John is already a land-owner with interest in a little sixteen-hundred-acre spread across the border in Oklahoma.

The other day John fell and broke an arm while swinging on some grapevine with his kids out on the Oklahoma place. He went in to Sherman to have the bone set.

"You're not one of *the* Waggoners, are you?" the doctor asked.

"Yep," John replied.

Then, thinking that the sawbones might gouge him good in the pocketbook, John quickly added, "But I'm not with the Vernon side of the family. We're the poorer relations down south a few counties."

Decatur, 1975

An Oilman

Loyd Powell could eat out at Mario's every night and fun away at the Fairmont, but he doesn't. Instead he's usually on some sorry stretch between Big D and Inadale, picking chicken-fry from his teeth and sizing up the seismic implication of some old anticlines the big boys have overlooked. For you boll weevils who don't know the oil patch, an anticline is a fault in the lay of the land, an upfold of rocks which to the experienced eye might indicate oil or gas sands. Texas has more anticlines than any place this side of the Sahara, and while they've been picked over and produced pretty good, there's plenty left if you've got the money and the time, not to speak of the pipe and piss and vinegar, to lose your ass trying to bring one in. These days you've got to be an indepedent son of a buccaneer to get away with it, and lucky, science being what it isn't. Loyd hasn't been so lucky of late.

Take this summer. One Saturday night in July, Loyd caught me at home and said, "Look, don't get so drunk tonight you can't get up in the morning."

"Whatcha got going?"

"I'll pick you up at four and we'll hit 'em to Palo Pinto County. My pusher just called from the rig and said they'll be hitting a little sand at twenty-two hundred feet, and I'd like to take a look at it."

Now, I hate to get up early as much as the next rooster, but I felt I had no choice. I knew how important this well was to Loyd. It was his first in six months, and hell, he had something like sixty thousand dollars in it. "Okay," I said, "I'll break my date and see you in the morning." And that's what I did. I called this beautiful blonde—her name is Erin and she's my fourteen-year-old daughter—and said, sorry honey, can't make it tonight. Can't take you to Shakey's for pasteboard and silent slapstick. I postponed again what was already a long overdue paroxysm of paternity. In Environmental America, old oilmen must stick together. It's kind of like the Masons. And my daddy was both, a driller and a secret riter. I dropped out of DeMolay, but I couldn't turn my back on memories of Longview, Glade-water, Kilgore, and Henderson. I went to bed early, with derricks dancing in my head.

Loyd, as usual, was on time.

With his damn dogs, Gretchen and Rex, two of the largest German shepherds in captivity. Celeste, Loyd's young bride, was away for the weekend, visiting her folks in San Antonio, and Loyd had orders not to leave the puppy-poohs alone. Gretchen would fast in protest. So the dogs reigned from the back seat of the Cadillac. This bothered me because I had invited Gary Bishop, the brilliant photographer, along, and I knew that Gary would be grumpy at such an hour and grumpier still at having to compress his loose and elongated frame into the leftover space. But Bishop is a pro and didn't bitch. He said later he was afraid the dogs would bite him.

To the west we rolled, out into the July dawn, through four counties and into another state of mind: the rural ennui of abandoned barns and absentee landlords, where wide spots in the road barely make a dent in the bumper of your mind. A Cadillac, even with giant, police-state dogs breathing down your neck, is a compelling conveyance. Quiet, sleek, heavy with power and luxury like having a Roman in torque and a Greek in attendance, it soothes your fears of the open road and of strange companions, and Loyd and Gary began to feel one another out.

Both are as timid of talking as Twain on the Chautauqua, but quite opposite characters, and they took some time to tune up. Loyd is an anachronism. In his manner and dress, in his ideas and values, he is a swashbuckler of the Texas fifties. He seems to have just stepped off a Trans-Texas prop plane from Austin, where he has been closeted at the capitol with Governor

Shivers and Price Daniel (the old man, not the boy), plotting to keep the Texas tidelands and throw Harry Truman out of office. Gary, on the other hand, looks like a male model's version of a chic *Cosmo* or *Playboy* photographer, all old denim and elegant equipment. Handsome and long-haired, he has to holster his Nikons and hide his good nature to keep the chicks away. They all want to undress for him and his art.

Here Loyd was the son of a rich roughneck, a scion of North Dallas, and Gary was out of a middle-class mechanic, a South Dallas success story, and already they had found a connective. Both had dated the same beautiful girl. Loyd had seen her first, back in high school, and you could tell that he thought she had gone downhill since then, running around with hippies and such, while Gary obviously saw her as liberated at last from the strictures of a banker's daughter's life. With that dichotomy and the dogs at the back of our minds, we musketeered the morning away, skirmishing on sports, religion, and politics, Loyd lamenting Nixon's plight and pointing out oil wells we passed, Gary grinning and shooting. We left Weatherford in our wake, passed through Mineral Wells like a laxative, geared down in Graford, and took the Jacksboro highway out to the Jim Green place, where, on a hill well behind the house, Loyd and the Carter Development Company had a double jackknife rig digging away.

Loyd had had a helluva time getting the lease and clearing a road to the spot where he wanted to drill. It was like riding over a washboard. One of the trucks hauling in the works had turned over in a gully, and now, as we bumped along, we came upon a stalled car. A big, red-faced man in a dirty straw hat was inside the hood, banging on a battery.

"That's my morning tower driller," Loyd said.

Ray Mardis was his name, out of Ranger. His Chevy had been in the oil patch almost as many years as Mardis had, and Loyd's jumper cables wouldn't rouse it. The rest of his crew had gone on in another car, so the driller rode with us to the rig and borrowed a truck to drive home.

The sun had already burned away the morning mist, and the rig sat there silent, silhouetted in the cloudless sky. The bit had worn out, so they had come out of the hole. The drill stem was stacked in the derrick. The daylight driller, Ralph Ramsey, another old roughneck from Ranger, was in the doghouse looking at the electric log. His crew was off the floor, out in the parking area banging on the back of a second-hand Cadillac. Loyd put leashes on Gretchen and Rex and let them out of the back seat. "Let's go to the powder room," he coaxed, and they dragged him off into the mesquite.

Gary gazed in wonder at the rig. He had never seen one.

A wiry little man with not a tooth in his head raised himself from the rear of the old Cadillac. "Say," he said, "Let's see if your key will fit my trunk."

"What's the problem?"

"Aw," he said, grinning, "We locked ourselves out and cain't get to the water jug in the trunk here. Just made a trip and 'bout to die of thirst."

Loyd emerged from the mesquite and handed him the keys. They didn't fit.

"Shit," the little roughneck said. His name was Leroy Jocoby. He was the derrick hand. After thirty-five years in the oil patch he had two used Cadillacs and a girl in Borger, and here he couldn't get a drink of water to save his soul.

Leroy shook his head and looked at the floor men, Chubby Smith and Derrell Teague. Chubby was a red giant, naked to the waist. He had broken in on his first rig back in '49 at Hadacol Corner, between Midland and Odessa, surely the meanest stretch of honky-tonks since Moonshine Hill. It was dead out there now, most of the big oil action gone. About all a man could do in the Permian Basin now was drink and fight and light farts and say "mother-fucker" every adjective. Chubby had a busted disc, nine fingers, seven ex-wives, and seven kids. His eighth wife, Jo Ann, who had also been his seventh, was driving the twenty miles from Mineral Wells to the rig to give Chubby his high blood pressure pills. He'd gotten dizzy coming out of the hole and had called her on the shortwave.

"How'm I gonna down a pill without water?" Chubby said. He looked at Derrell. Derrell was the boll weevil, the inexperienced member of the crew, but he looked like he had been throwing pig iron around all his life. His biceps were so big they were bursting through his shirt. Derrell laughed and looked at me, and I laughed and looked at Loyd, and Loyd frowned and looked at the dogs. "I'll tie 'em to a tree," he said, "and we'll go get you some water."

We drove over to a post oak grove about half a mile away where the evening tower driller, Estel Martin, had his camp. Martin's crew consisted of his son, D. W., Estel's brother, Willard, and Willard's boy, Willard, Jr. Some pickups, a camper, and a trailer house were arranged in a circle like covered wagons in Indian territory, and when we drove up the women and kids scattered like chickens.

Estel Martin stood his ground. He was littler than Leroy. "What do you want?" he said flatly. Loyd explained. Martin didn't say anything. He just whirled and went and got a water can and handed it to Loyd. "We'll need our own water tonight," he said.

"I'll have 'em refill it," Loyd assured him.

Gary was clicking away with his Nikon. Martin caught him out of the corner of his eye. "Hey," he said, turning on Gary. "Better be careful with them pictures."

"You don't want your picture taken?"

"No," Martin said. And we tiptoed away.

Back at the rig Loyd watered the men and the dogs and assayed the sand at twenty-two hundred feet. He looked at the Schlumberger log, sniffed the samples, talked to the driller, and talked to himself. "Porosity, porosity," he said over and over. "It boils down to if you've got porosity."

He wasn't going for oil; he smelled gas. He felt he was in the same structure as the Halsell No. 14, a good gas producer that had been drilled six years before. The Halsell was forty-three hundred feet to the south. Of course to the north, nineteen hundred feet away, was the Lillie Humphries No. 1, the wildcatter of the field which had been drilled fourteen years before and was a dry hole. You take your chances. Loyd had gotten as close as he could. He told Ramsey to put on a new bit, a seventeen-hundred-dollar Howard Hughes sealed bearing special, and go on down to twenty-seven hundred feet. Could be some development there. Slim, but worth a look.

So they cranked her up, the Jim Green 1-A. Leroy went up in the derrick, Ralph Ramsey took control at the works, cat-head chain awhipping, and Chubby and Derrell stood over the hole and went at the pipe hammer and tong, stringing it together for the trip in. The red Waukesha diesels roared, the rig groaned and shook, and the kelly joint went up and down, picking up pipe and putting it into the hole until they touched bottom. They took off the kelly and put it in the mouse hole. Ralph eased off on the bull wheel and let the bit on bottom rotate. Now they were drilling.

"Call me at twenty-seven hundred," Loyd said, and we went back to Dallas.

That was on July 21.

Within ten days, Loyd had bad news on two fronts. First, John Connally, the best friend the oilman ever had in Washington, was indicted for taking a bribe. That was on the twenty-ninth. On the thirty-first, Loyd plugged the Jim Green 1-A at forty-four hundred feet—gave it up as a dry hole.

At times in the past few years Loyd Powell wondered if his inheritance was worth it, that maybe it was more curse than blessing. It was as if some ancient ancestor, a Zeus of a man, had sent anachronistic tendencies tailing off into the generations like time bombs, and Loyd was one of the wounded, a victim of genetic shrapnel. Yet he had only to look back one paternity to see the source. For it was not the money and the responsibility to carry on that bothered him, but rather the predilection and passion of his father so apparent within him. He looked more like his mother than his father, but he was definitely the old man's son. They both loved to squint into the sun. And that was the problem. It was one thing to be L. W. Powell, drilling contractor and independent oil operator in the boom days of East Texas, and quite another to be Loyd Walter Powell, Jr., second-generation oilman in Environmental America. Loyd was of this age all right—hell, he was under thirty—but he didn't feel in it.

He wanted action, not soul-searching psychology. Life was to conquer, not to contemplate, and Loyd's head was full of stories of his father's heyday.

It musta been around '28 or '29. I was down in the Hendricks field in Winkler County—biggest discovery in West Texas—working as production foreman for the Southern Crude Oil Purchasing Company. That was a subsidiary of the Standard of Indiana. Well, Sid Richardson come in there with an old cable tool rig and they'd have trouble fishing, losing their tools in the hole, lines breaking, jars breaking. At that time there wasn't any rotary rigs out in there until we brought ours in. They said we could never drill our well with a rotary. Why hell, we had ours in production before they got out from under the surface. But Sid never would give up on his old cable tool. He kept drilling and fishing. Well, finally one day he come up to me and said he needed a drilling line. I said, "Well, we got some in stock." So I called the office and they never did say whether I could let him have it or not. I knew he was broke and in trouble, so I said go ahead and take the line, and if anything comes up I'll tell 'em you will replace it. I think we delivered it for him. Anyway, a few days later Red Iron was out there. At that time Red was general superintendent, the man over me, and I told him about it and he said, "Aw, that's all right. We've got some acreage around him and we've given him some bottom hole money, some dry hole money. If he gets a well he proves out our acreage."

So from then on I guess we rebuilt the rig for him, and he got a nice well. As far as I know, that was Sid's start to the top.

The last time I talked to him I ran into him there in Fort Worth and he said, "Powell, what are you doing?" That was back when I was drilling and I said, "Oh, just another broke contractor, trying to make a living." He says, "Wanna go to work for me?" I says, "Oh, I can't work for you." And he says, "Hell, I'll buy you rigs and let you pick your job."

And you didn't do it, Daddy.

And I didn't do it.

And aren't you glad?

Well shoot, boy, Sid Richardson, he made a lot of money. But he was that type of feller you know. If you ever helped him, why he never forgot it.

They a big company, one of the richest in the world.

You know that's where John Connally got started. He was Sid's lawyer and right-hand man. Now that Connally. He's something. I like him. He's a friend to the oilman if there ever was one.

It seemed a bolder, more adventurous time, more manly, somehow, than his own, and for a while there Loyd felt cramped at every turn of his growing maturity, a Gulliver in a land of Lilliputians. Going down to the office in the Exchange Bank Building just made it worse. He would sit there choking on his tie, rearing to go with no place to go and nothing to do that he really wanted to do. Here he was, an oily son of machinery and motion, stuck twelve stories high in downtown Dallas, hemmed in by paper money men and Ross Perot robots, when really his heart was out in East Texas on a drilling rig floor, spudding in and drilling, logging and notching, swabbing and coring and perforating, hitting a dry hole or bringing in a well, it didn't matter—just goddamn doing something!

The way they did in the old days. Sure it was dangerous, clamorous work that left them muddy and greasy and worn out after a twelve-hour tour, but God, it was worth it. In every boll weevil and honky-tonk waitress there was a wildcat streak that said you went out and got it while the getting was good. You didn't worry about being laid off or hung over; that would take care of itself. Hell, wages were good, and the oil sands stretched as far as a little financing and a good rock hound and Miss Lady Luck could take the bossman. A forty-hour work week and fringe benefits were scoffed at by drilling men. You paid a man for working, not for the time off and in between. Anywhere there was oil there was excitement.

Take a crossroads like Moonshine Hill, just outside Humble, Texas. Forty saloons and twenty thousand roughnecks in tents. H. Henry Cline, who used to fire boilers, remembered walking down the mud-mired main street and counting six fist-fights. W. H. Bennett, the old doctor at Humble, once said he made a "right smart a-livin' " treating roughnecks for knife and gunshot wounds. Not to speak of the clap. Ross Sterling might have remained a feed store proprietor out there if oil hadn't been struck. As it was, he ended up founding the mighty Humble Oil & Refining Company and becoming governor of Texas.

Those were the boom days they refused to believe would end. Sure, fields dried up or ran out of drilling room; that was an axiom as old as Colonel Drake and Watson's Flat. But if you couldn't strike it anymore in Pennsylvania, you went to West Virginia, Ohio, Kentucky, California, *Texas* and *Oklahoma!* And so it went, through a hundred years and thirty-two states and 213 Texas counties, until something like six hundred thousand gas and oil wells had been brought in and tapped.

Loyd was the first to admit that they had been money-hungry adventurers, but hell, they were also trying to stay ahead of an insatiable and growing demand for petroleum products, not only in the United States but the world over. Every index in America was rising: more people, more jobs, more businesses, more houses and cars and trains and ships and planes. We came roaring out of World War I the most powerful and industrial nation on earth, and we went charging into the century's new prosperity with the same gusto and abandon that had marked our exploration of the continent the hundred years before.

J. Frank Dobie, that deceptive cowboy of campus and chaparral, once summed up the American spirit in this way: In the Old World, he said, the legends that persisted with the most vitality were legends of women—Venus, Helen of Troy, Dido, Guinevere, Joan of Arc. But in the New World men have been neither lured or restrained by women. It has been a world of men exploring unknown continents, subduing wildernesses and savage tribes, butchering buffalo, trailing millions of longhorn cattle wilder than buffalo, digging gold out of mountains, pumping oil out of the hot earth beneath the plains. Into this world women have hardly entered except as realities; the idealizations, the legends, have been about great wealth to be found —the wealth of secret mines and hidden treasures, a wealth that is solid and has nothing to do with ephemeral beauty.

That was the way it had been, the way Loyd looked back on it. A saga. Restless, with raw appetites that grew in number as they were refined, we built industrial America! It excited him to think about it, there in his carpeted cubicle.

Loyd had come along a little too late. By 1955, the year he was nine and fell into one of his father's mud pits, the oil industry of Texas and the Southwest was settling into pokey middle age. Most of the fabulous fields had just about been drilled up, and the leases were left to workover crews and roustabouts, to the pumpers and switchers who tried to wring the last drop out of an old gusher. Nursemaids really. Out in the Permian Basin you couldn't even get into a fight.

The real men, the explorers, had moved on to where the new play was developing—to Wyoming, Alaska, the Australian Outback, and the Sahara Desert. And it was the kind of action that was too big and expensive for the independents, unless they gave up and went in with the majors like Humble. Not only was the easy oil in Texas harder to find, it was getting damned expensive to drill and produce. Costs of men and materials had gone up faster than crude oil prices. Of course the industry had men in Austin and Washington to protect them—governors like Allan Shivers and John Connally, congressmen like Sam Rayburn and Oklahoma's Robert S. Kerr, and even Lyndon Baines Johnson—but most of the special favors, federal tax relief, and state limits on production seemed to help the majors more than the little man. And it was the little man, the independent, who was doing most of the drilling and taking the losses on dry holes. And, damn, you got a dry hole about 38 percent of the time.

Loyd's daddy used to tell him that an oilman could go up quicker and come down faster than any other breed of man, and old L. W. was living proof. Out in East Texas and on the plains he and Red Iron had gone in together on a shoestring with another fella, and before they knew it they were worth half a million. Then Red fooled around and lost it on some wells in Mississippi, and suddenly they were broke. "Red," L. W. said, "I know you're in bad shape, so I'm gonna give you my stock and start over."

They shook hands on it, but before they parted, Red, with understandable embarrassment, told L. W. that he had to have five hundred dollars to pay his grocery bill. L. W. went to the Gladewater bank and borrowed the money, telling Red to pay him back when he struck it rich again. They found Red dead one morning not long after. He had a heart attack while reading the *Dallas Morning News*. The Japanese had attacked Pearl

Harbor, and President Roosevelt was declaring war. L. W. was forty-one, but he enlisted.

When he got out he married a Nacogdoches school teacher, Reba Jo, and went back to drilling on contract. After a time he got him a stake and started operating as an independent. He knew the technical side of the business—by this time he had drilled more than two thousand wells—so he bought his own portable rigs and ran them, and as the wells were brought in and producing, L. W. kept a crew of roustabouts to look after them and the tanks. He set up headquarters in the Exchange Bank Building in Dallas, hired Robert Bozman as his accountant, and stationed his field superintendent, Arnold Rohmer, in Muenster just below the Red River and the Oklahoma border, where much of his production was.

By the time L. W. decided it was time to let Loyd take over, he had about two hundred wells in Texas and Oklahoma. That was in 1969, when Loyd got out of the army. All told, since January of this year the Powell wells have produced more than 6.3 million barrels of oil and 5 billion cubic feet of gas. That's not in H. L. Hunt's league, but it's pretty high octane company for a poor boy from Smiley. And L. W. did it without the services of a single geologist. Instead of geology, he practiced what he calls closeology, laying back and waiting for a wildcatter to prove a field before he went in with his rig. Closeology was simply spudding in as close to a producing well as the law and the landowners would allow. Of course he had to pay more to get a lease, but it increased his chances of making a well. And it made him a rich man.

Today he and Reba Jo have a beautiful home in North Dallas, but you can usually find L. W. up at the family ranch between Muenster and Saint Joe, chomping on a cigar and riding herd on the ranch hands. The Powell place embraces five thousand acres of rolling hill and valley, rich with thirty-eight varieties of grass and fat with black Angus and Brahma cattle. It is a paying ranch and not a tax write-off since L. W. quit killing himself raising world-champion Appaloosa horses. The old man, who is seventy-four, had his second heart attack at the ranch three years ago. Loyd happened to be there. He helped his father to his Cadillac, gunned the engine, and covered the eighty-nine miles to Dallas and the hospital in fifty minutes. "Ever' once in a while," L. W. recalled, "I'd allow myself a look at the speedometer. That boy had the needle on a hundred."

Loyd had no illusions on his coming of age as an oilman.

There was no sense in pretending he was starting from scratch like his old man. It was a rich man's game now, no matter where you drilled or how deep. His father had gone to the University of Hard Knocks so that Loyd could have the privilege of private school (St. Mark's in Dallas) and university (University of Denver, SMU School of Business), and he was not entirely on his own and accountable only to himself. The old man kept some of the action and was free with his advice. His sister was in for a percentage, so they incorporated and called themselves the L&M Oil Company (for Loyd and Mary). Mary was married to a doctor and wouldn't be taking an active interest, so Loyd had a fairly free hand.

Of course there were others to consider: the old family friend and accountant, Robert Bozman, and the backers that Loyd would bring in on each venture. Some operators never put their own money into a well, but Loyd didn't believe in that. If he got a dry hole he wanted to be able to tell his partners that he was out some, too—sometimes 25 percent and maybe even 75 percent. He had one other rule. He wouldn't ask a man to invest unless that man could stand to lose ten or twenty thousand. Because you had to go in prepared to lose. Geology, which you had to have now, was no guarantee, and it improved your chances of a strike by only a few percentage points. It was a high-risk business that only the established could afford. Once you had a well, however, it was self-perpetuating and profitable for a long time. Usually. That wasn't always true. But the Powells' oldest producing well, McKinley No. 1, had been pumping since 1938, the second best well they've ever had.

And this was the other rather sobering thing about Loyd's ascension. Unless something really bizarre happened, he would have to content himself with poking through leftover oil patches. Oh, he would drill a wildcat once in a while, but it would be highly unlikely that Loyd Powell would ever open up something like a Spindletop or a Scurry Reef. None of this rankology for him. It didn't mean that most of the oil was gone. There was more down there than had ever been taken out, but it was deep and difficult to get to and would have to await new technology. One of the most spectacular dry holes of modern times was an attempt, in 1958 and 1959, to find oil at twenty-five thousand feet in Pecos County. Loyd would go for shallow sands and play his old man's game of closeology. He would also have to pick his way through a complex system of regulations and price controls that would have baffled the old-timers. Between locating a lease and bringing in a well there would be mountains of paperwork and many middlemen with which to deal.

The days of a handshake confirming a contract were over, gone with the likes of that great Ft. Worth cavalier, Jack Grace. Even into the fifties, Grace insisted on sealing a deal by shaking hands and looking you in the eye. Once he and J. Langford Shaw had come to terms over the phone, but Grace, never having met Shaw, insisted on flying out to Sherman to see him. Shaw was at the airport when Grace's Beechcraft landed. Grace came down the ramp, shook Shaw's hand, exchanged a pleasantry, and was gone within five minutes, winging his way back to Fort Worth. "I just wanted to look that fella in the eye," he explained to his pilot.

So much of that romance was gone. Well, Loyd was prepared for it. But what he was not prepared for was an almost sudden change of mood in the American people's attitude toward industry in general and oilmen in particular. In 1969, the year Loyd set himself up at his father's desk, public resentment at the fouling of our air and water took legislative form in the National Environment Policy Act, which toughened licensing requirements for nuclear and fossil fuel plants. Conservationists joined the environmentalists, and pretty soon people were saying, shame! look what the industrialists and developers have done—they had taxed the body of the continent until the land itself, the good earth, was showing definite signs of depletion. People like the Powells had gone to the well too many times.

The domestic oilman was down in the dumps anyway, and

this criticism didn't do him any good. Prices were down, costs were up, and operators began to get out of the business just as Loyd was coming into it. Manufacturers stopped making tools. Oil field supply houses began closing. Related service industries began laying off people. Domestic exploration declined as oil imports increased. It seemed to Loyd that the media played up oil spills and ecological damage from pipeline construction. L. W. Powell had been pictured as a producer, a provider. Loyd hated to seem paranoid, but he got the distinct impression that polluter and exploiter were the new appellatives for his kind. Every time he picked up a newspaper or a magazine, some energy expert was predicting that we were running out of fossil fuels, that we had better conserve while converting to new forms of energy. Natural gas would be gone in thirty years, oil in maybe a hundred.

Well, the Texas Railroad Commission was indeed prorating production, keeping it down to a few days a month. While around the world, and even in other states, the big companies were allowed to pump their wells at full blast. It seemed to Loyd that the independent in Texas was being choked to death in the name of conservation. The incentive to drill just wasn't there, and in the first four years of his stewardship he attempted only a dozen wells. He was getting about $3.25 or $3.65 a barrel, which on the inflation scale amounted to a whole lot less than the $2.50 a barrel his dad was getting in 1955. He had two gas wells out in West Central Texas he couldn't even connect. One hundred thousand dollars sunk in two shut-in wells. The market out there was interstate and therefore regulated by the Federal Power Commission, and the FPC kept the price of gas so low Loyd couldn't afford to sell it. He'd never get his money back. As far as he was concerned, the industry was like a balloon with the air let out of it. Loyd spent a lot of time out on the ranch guzzling Dr. Peppers and staring at the stock, and he wasn't that turned on by beef.

One day he told his drilling contractor, Stumpy Stevens, that, damn it, he felt like a tit on a boar hog. Useless. Vestigial. Hell, Stumpy knew what he meant. He was hurting, too. Why, he would throw in a string of free surface pipe if Loyd would let him drill a well. Free this, free that. It was just like when there were a lot of apartments in Dallas. The managers would give you a month's free rent and throw in a couple of go-go girls on the side. Hmmm.

Old L. W. listened and wondered if maybe the ranch might prove to be a better bonanza for the boy than all that oil and pig iron. Now that he had gotten rid of his horses he was finding a tranquility in the country, in grass and grain and trees and cows and water, that he had never found tracking down oil leases and drilling. It was a high-pressure business, the oil field, and L. W. worried that Loyd worried so much. It would kill him if he didn't relax. Loyd was single, but he didn't play like you would expect. He wore a Stetson and drove an Eldorado, but he was no high roller. As a matter of fact, Loyd was careful with his money, maybe too careful. Of course these were peculiar times. A man had to be patient.

And sure enough, Loyd's luck turned.

First in the shape of a little beauty from San Antonio. Celeste Altgelt was her name. Fine old German family. Insurance and ranching.

Loyd and Celeste hadn't been married but a few months when the October War between the Israelis and the Arabs broke out. The Arabs, of course, put an embargo on oil shipments to the United States, and quicker'n you could say seismic, the situation changed. America was screaming for oil to meet the energy crisis, and all the talk of profligate producers went down the drain of dry gas tanks. Production allowables were raised to all the pipes could bear, and local oilmen started walking tall again.

Loyd Powell put it in high gear. He hadn't drilled in fourteen months, but now, in quick succession, he dug two—first a wildcat that was as dry as a mummy's tomb, and then a gas well that Loyd decided to shut in until the government let the price go up. The dry-hole wildcat cost Loyd and his partners eighty thousand dollars; the latent gas well was sixty thousand.

Oil had jumped up to ten dollars a barrel, but damn it, there was talk in Congress of a crude oil price rollback. One day in February Loyd called in his secretary, Della Blankenship, and dictated a telegram to Senator Henry M. Jackson in Washington. He warned the senator that a price rollback would be disastrous and counterproductive, that marginal wells would have to be plugged again, and that independents would be discouraged from further exploration. A month and eight days later, Senator Jackson replied by letter:

> While I recognize the role of higher prices in stimulating the development of new oil supplies, I also recognize the need to protect the consumer and the economy from the impact of excessive price increases for petroleum products. The Committee's hearings and investigations make clear that there is no justification for the unprecedented price increases for crude oil and petroleum products in recent months.

The senator went on to add that he was proposing legislation to put a ceiling on crude oil. Loyd made copies of Jackson's letter and mailed them to his various backers, adding his own comment that Jackson was ignorant when it came to the oil business. "I wonder," Loyd closed, "when Henry Jackson put his money where his mouth is and invested in a wildcat?"

Loyd didn't drill for six months. It wasn't because he didn't want to. He had seventy thousand dollars tied up in leases and was anxious to prove a pocketful of other prospects. His problem was pipe. It was hard to get. Domestic drilling had stepped up 25 percent, and the steel companies weren't prepared for the demand. Besides, they were committed to foreign producers. Loyd kept hearing stories of black market pipe stacked to the ceiling in warehouses owned by brokers, of a Cajun in Louisiana getting iron from Spain, but actually finding it was as hard as striking an oil sand. He had Rohmer and the boys pull fifty-four hundred feet of casing out of an old well in East Texas, and he got some sucker rods and some surface pipe, but hell, he still needed one hundred thousand feet of tubing, just more of everything.

And then he got it, just enough to start, and in July he sunk that sixty thousand dollars into the Palo Pinto dry hole Gary Bishop photographed. What did he do? He and the Carter

Company moved the rig to another site a few miles away, and of this writing, Loyd's latest well is registering one hundred thousand feet of gas pressure, so he may have something. It's not fantastic, but at least a little encouragement.

And Loyd's not complaining. The oil business right now looks better to him than it ever has in his memory. If the government will just leave it alone and the majors don't mash them into the ground. The big explorers are starting to come back home, now that they are finding foreign governments more hostile. Loyd is so optimistic he has moved L&M into the new Energy Center complex north of downtown. There, he and Bozman and Mrs. Blankenship are surrounded by other oilmen who share their excitement. Someone is even setting up a geology library. Loyd is back and forth between the field and the office, his pockets full of lease agreements, his valise full of maps, and his belly full of chicken-fried steak. He loves to read what he calls the Bible of the industry, *The Oil and Gas Journal*, and to pore over what he calls the Dun & Bradstreet of the industry, *The Oil Directory of Texas and Production Survey*. The directory separates the men from the boys, and it fascinates Loyd. The other day at the office he was feeling pretty good. He had a new pair of Nocona boots, and Celeste was at Neiman's having her hair streaked. They were getting ready to make the river fiesta in San Antonio. Loyd bent over the directory and went through its pages in a random fashion.

"Boy, there's some real stories in here. What you can do is look at this year's book, and then look at last year's, and you can see whether they're up or down. Our gas is holding about the same, but our oil is down some. But there're some people in here you've never heard of! I don't even know who they are. Like this guy here, John Cox out of Midland. I don't know where he comes from or who he is or anything. He got over 403,000 barrels a month; that's a little over 13,000 barrels a day, and that's a hell of a lot of money. I don't know how much of that he actually owns.

"Ah, here's a little company called Cokinos. It's a fun company just gettin' started. There's a lot of little companies. I don't know. The Kennedys're in here under some little com-

pany. Can't remember what they call it. Just getting started. Lot
of stories in here. Gonna be some better ones. Risky maybe, but
a lot of romance. It's just exciting to go out and drill you a well
and smell you oil nobody's ever found. It's been there for millions and millions of years, and ever' drop you find goes into the
national oil stream and supplies a guy in North Carolina with
five gallons to go see his grandmother. And we're ridiculed so
bad. But that's just one of the things you have to accept. We're
in the minority and always will be."

Dallas, 1974

The Stone That Cries
Like a Child

Goyo Maldonado stopped coming to church after he found the Stone That Cries Like a Child.

The padre, Joseph Daspit, suspected the reason for Goyo's absence, for he had heard the story of the stone and its mysterious powers. But he decided to be patient. Goyo's wife, Lupe, still came to Mass. Perhaps the woman would bring him back. The priest, a Vincentian, had served these people for many years, and he knew the strength of their women.

Winter's last wind swept through Cotulla with a tumbleweed broom and lost itself in the moaning chaparral. It was late in the spring, after the rains when the Christweeds were sweet with their bloody blooms, before Father Joe noticed that Lupe Maldanado was not in her pew in the little Church of the Sacred Heart.

That afternoon he knocked at the door of Goyo's house in Mexican Town.

Lupe came to the door. "Oh Father," she whispered and cast down her eyes.

"I wish to speak with Goyo," he said.

Lupe nodded, but she did not tell him that her house was his. She left him on the porch and went for her husband.

Goyo, a small, brown man of middle age, appeared in the doorway. He was a *cholo*, and his clothes were as worn and crude as his hands.

"It makes many months . . . ," Father Joe began.

"Yes," Goyo said. He did not avoid the padre's eyes as Lupe had done. But the priest could not read his face. It was a blank mask.

"Goyo, I've come to see La Piedra Que Llora Como un Niño."

"Forgive me, Father," Goyo replied. And he shut the door.

La Piedra Que Llora Como un Niño, the stone that cries like a child. It was a strange tale, one that appealed to a simple folk's feel for fantasy in this sun-blistered, blunt country. In the hot little houses and warm-beer cantinas they talked of how Goyo had found the stone.

Goyo and Lupe had been picking prickly pear in a pasture when Goyo stumped his toe on a stone. To his astonishment, the stone cried like a child. He knelt before it in fear, and the stone spoke, in the lamblike voice of a *niño,* and calmed his heart with its story. It had once been a human child, abandoned on the roadside to die. But God took pity and turned it to stone. It had lain there for a time beyond measure, waiting for someone to come for it. Whoever would take it and keep it would bring joy and good fortune into their house. Goyo and Lupe, whose house was barren of child, took the round, bright black rock home in their arms.

Goyo, who all his life had been a common *cholo,* a grubber of chaparral and burner of cactus, became something of an *adivino,* a diviner, for it was said that the stone passed on supernatural powers to its keeper.

When some of the townspeople began to go to Goyo for advice and prophecy, Father Joe put on his thinking cap.

The padre decided it was time for *las visitas de la Virgen Peregrina,* the visits of the Pilgrim Virgin, a fine old Catholic custom. First, the priest polishes up the church's finest statue of the Virgin Mary for a visit to the homes of the faithful. Each deserving family gets to keep the Pilgrim Mary for one day, then passes the statue on to another equally deserving household. The stigma that falls on the house that is skipped, *por Dios,* is something devoutly to be avoided.

The house of Goyo, of course, was not honored with a *visita de la Virgen Peregrina.* The house to the left of Goyo was blessed with Her Presence, as was the house to his right. In fact, all the houses on the street had Her—all save one.

The good and shrewd Father Joe let the lesson sink in; then, with the chalk Mary in his strong arms, he tapped on Goyo's door.

"Goyo," he said, "I come with the Pilgrim Mary. She wants to honor your house."

A great relief seemed to come over Goyo's old face. You know Lupe had been giving him hell. "Gracias, Padre, gracias," he cried, and reached for the statue.

"*Un momento,*" Father Joe said, crossing himself, "you give me the Stone That Cries Like a Child and I will give you the Blessed Virgin."

Goyo told the priest to keep the statue and closed the door.

"This all happened many years ago," Father Joe said. He rubbed his eyes with thick, red-freckled fingers and let his big body sink back in the swivel chair.

"I left Cotulla not long after and was gone for many years. By the time I returned, Goyo and Lupe were dead, I suppose from natural causes, and the whole thing had been forgotten. I don't know what happened to the Stone That Cries Like a Child, or, as some called it, El Niño Perdido de la Piedra Negra, the Lost Child of the Black Rock.

"But I tell the story to illustrate the peculiar religious sense of the Mexican. It isn't necessarily connected with piety or regular church attendance, because I've seen it in those who won't go to church.

"It isn't something acquired, or at least I don't think it is. They seem to be born with an awareness, or at least a suscepti-bility, a sensitivity to spiritual forces.

"Maybe it comes with being poor for so long. They sense there is more to this world than what meets the eye.

"Now take this goat herder who came in and asked for a

wooden crucifix; not a plastic crucifix, not a metal one could I sell him. It had to be of *madera,* wood.

"But oh, that's a long story. The hour is late and the señora has my supper ready. You come back *mañana,* okay?"

Chuy Reyes, University of Corpus Christi, class of '61, opened the bottle of beer and set it on the counter of his father's café.

"Sure," he said with a grin. "I've heard the story. It's a good one, huh? But come on, guy, you don't expect me to believe that rock really talked, do you?"

Cotulla, 1965

The Last Spring of
Our Innocence

In 1940 Tommy Grisham ran away to Dallas to room and board
with his Aunt Ida. None of us was certain Ida Ballard was his
real aunt, but she treated him better than all the other foster
families he had tried. Tommy stayed with her until he went
away to war. That was Tommy's big thing, to get into the war.
He was a big, fat, nervous kid who was still wetting the bed the
last time I saw him, which was the summer of '44. We were
never sure of his exact age, except that we figure he lied, added
a little so the marines would take him.

Mrs. Ballard lived in a little frame house on Poe Avenue.
It was never a rich man's street, but it offered a tree-shaded sta-
bility to the working middle class. It was the only real home
Tommy ever had, and he used to show off the neighborhood as
if he had lived there all his life. In October at state fair time I
would come up from South Texas, and at dusk Tommy would
take me from house to house, pointing at the pale lights and
the people within, telling me as much as he knew about them.
There was Effie Spence, who, like Aunt Ida, was a widow
woman. For years Effie and her husband Eugene ran the barbecue stand around the corner on North Haskell. L. G. and Win-
nie White were across the street. L. G. was the manager at Dixie
Electric, and Tommy claimed that Mr. White had wired the
Flying Red Horse, the tallest thing in the Dallas skyline—had
wired it for lights, Mr. White had, and Gawd, was it gorgeous!
Which it was. Next door were the Travers, J. E. and Mary. J. E.
was a bank cashier. And then there were Dick and Ethel Barnes,
Annie Early, John Roach the mailman, and Hubert Wynn, an
engineer. Their kids went to North Dallas High School.

The classroom rolls over the years included Earle Cabell, Eugene Locke, Barefoot Sanders, and every other kid in that part of town except Tommy Grisham. How he remained truant that long without getting caught is a testament to orphan ingenuity. No one claimed him, and he took advantage of it. Aunt Ida treated him like an adult. Which, in a way, he was. While other adolescents suffered the slings and arrows of education, Tommy cooled it at the ice house and fraternized with tramps at the freight yards. He pulled tickets at the Palace and was the kid you dunked into the water tank with baseball bull's-eyes at the fairground carnival. The banes of childhood were study hall, spinach, spankings, castor oil, and the fear of polio, none of which Tommy had to endure. He did neat things, like getting up at daybreak to deliver the *Morning News*. He sold subscriptions to *Grit*, the weekly that had a million readers, and peddled *Boy's Life* and *The Open Road for Boys*. He smoked yellow john and grapevine and chewed tobacco and peed in wine bottles to leave for stumblebums, all very manly stuff. If he could have stopped the bed-wetting I would have taken him at his word, but I had to lie in it when I was around.

Tommy was a kid, too. And Saturday was kid day. In the mornings we lay around reading comic books and listening to the radio serials such as "Jack Armstrong, the All-American Boy." In the afternoons we went to the neighborhood movie matinee. First Buster Crabbe and then Johnny Weissmuller was Tarzan, and then Crabbe donned a space suit to play Flash Gordon. We drank Barq's root beer and chewed Peter Paul's Activated Charcoal Gum. None of us took naps or vitamins, but bit into candy confections such as Joe Boy, a pink nugent center with caramel around it and a chocolate and peanut coating.

Sundays were for church, Mother's or Aunt Ida's fried chicken, and the "funnies," the Sunday comics from the *Times-Herald* or *News*. I never missed Major Hoople in "Our Boarding House," and Tommy liked the "Katzenjammer Kids." They were the meanest brats in comics. And of course there was "Little Orphan Annie," which Tommy didn't like.

Aunt Ida always read the advertisements aloud. "Well I

swan! Ham's up to twenty-nine cents a pound. Lordy me!" You could get three bars of Ivory for twenty-nine cents, three pounds of Crisco for sixty-eight, and bacon for thirty-nine cents a pound at the A&P. Neiman's was always high as a cat's back, Ida used to say. On that May of '44, the Saturday before Mother's Day, the Marcuses offered hand-done linens of organdy at forty-five dollars a set. Once in a while, if Aunt Ida felt expansive, she would let Tommy take the little Ford sedan out of the garage and warm it up, and then we would go for a Sunday evening drive, ending up for supper at the Rockyfeller Hamburger System.

You could not buy a pizza in Dallas. We would have to wait for the G.I.'s to come home from Italy with their new-found taste in bread and beauties with names like Gina and Sophia. Charles Scalise claims to be the originator of the pizza in Dallas, and he did not open his Campisi Egyptian Restaurant until 1946. How an Italian restaurant got an Egyptian name is not worth going into at this point, but as Harry Golden says, it could happen only in America.

Every night of the week was for radio. There was no T.V. What else was there not anything of? No freeways, no rock 'n' roll, no integration. After supper we would gather in a semi-circle and listen to Kay Kyser and his "College of Musical Knowledge," sponsored by Lucky Strike, the strongest cigarettes my old man ever smoked—stronger than Camels, he claimed. Or it would be Bob Hope for Pepsodent or Bing Crosby for Kraft. We loved "Fibber McGee and Molly," the "Lux Radio Theatre," hosted by Cecil B. De Mille, "Inner Sanctum," and, of course, being country folk who sang through our noses, Saturday night's "Grand Ole Opry" from Nashville.

I first heard a symphony orchestra play when we tuned in to Arturo Toscanini conducting the NBC Symphony, and I came to know a president from his fireside chats on radio. Franklin Delano Roosevelt made nearly three hundred radio talks, and I guess we heard most of them. He had been president longer than any man. There was as much comfort in his voice, through the depression and into the war years, as there was later to be in the voices of Edward R. Murrow and now Walter Cronkite.

In spite of the war, even adults were innocent then, at least those stateside. All the sins were sins of the flesh, like messing with tacky girls or mixing with the colored. When carhops got pregnant, they slipped off to the Edna Gladney Home in Fort Worth. When blacks got on the bus, they went to the back. It hadn't been long since the uppity ones were flogged in the Trinity River bottoms. Everything was smaller then: people, planes, places, perspectives on civil rights. Everything except patriotism. We still saw America as evidence on earth of the Promised Land, a glorious secular manifestation of Kingdom Come. We were on a bee-line of divine purpose from Genesis to Judgement Day to D-day and Heaven—or hell, as the case might be.

War was hell, but it was also fun, as Tommy Grisham and I saw it in the summer of '44. He kept in his room a clipping from the Fort Worth *Star-Telegram*, dated July 20, 1941. It was a byline story by one Frank X. Tolbert describing the boot camp experience of the New York Giants football star, Jack Lummus. Lummus was our own homegrown luminary, a six-foot, four-inch blond son of the Ennis town constable. He had starred at Baylor before joining the Giants. Now, with the sneak attack on Pearl Harbor fresh in American minds, sportswriters had flocked to Hicks Field to see Jack's initiation into the marines. In Tolbert's story he picked up on the play between Lummus and his commanding officer, Captain J. T. Biggs.

"Sound off," barked Biggs.

"I am Jack Lummus, formerly of Baylor University, Sir."

"Famous for what?"

"Famous for reciting one of Edna St. Vincent Millay's poems while seated on a cake of ice, Sir."

"What is a dodo?"

"A dodo is a large bird which flies in steadily decreasing concentric circles . . . ," Lummus went on.

Such a scene was of course to become a cliché repeated over and over again in reality and in the cartoons and radio and television shows and movies depicting raw recruits in the rite of soldiering. Specifically, however, Lummus's induction was to have a profound effect on the lives of three boys from Jack's hometown.

After reading Tolbert's story, Joe Crow, James Goodwin, and Tom Pierce vowed to join the marines the following summer after their graduation from Ennis High. Joe was simply Joe, but James was known as Airdale, and Tom's nickname was Dooney. They were all underage, but their parents came with them to Dallas to enlist. Their big dream was to stick together through the war and maybe end up in the same outfit with Jack Lummus.

Tommy Grisham didn't know the three boys from Ennis, but he had a similar idea. He was frantic to join before the war was over, but he had two obstacles to overcome: the down on his cheeks and the baby fat that betrayed his age. He conquered the first by shaving twice a day. He burned off the fat by placing himself in the mail-order hands of the world's most perfectly developed man, Charles Atlas.

Strong men and a single strong woman ruled the imagination of my youth. Thumb through the *Time* covers of the years between 1939 and 1945, and it is the faces of the emphatic who made "Man of the Year"—people like Barrymore and Ben-Gurion, Al Capone and Madame Chiang Kai-shek, Gary Cooper and Churchill, Doolittle and Dwight Eisenhower, Franco, Hitler, Hearst and Tom Harmon, Kilroy and Kai-shek (the Madame), Mussolini and MacArthur and Madame Chiang Kai-shek. It was a muscular, put-up-your-dukes gallery, and what it says is that Henry Luce, the *Time* publisher, had a thing for Chiang's wife. What is also says is that a ninety-seven-pound weakling didn't have a chance in those *Times*, even though men and women as a rule were smaller than they are today. The 1944 girl of stage, screen, radio, kitchen, and kinder stood five feet, three and one-half inches tall. She was longer in the leg, thicker in the waist (26.4 inches), and had slightly heavier hips (37.4 inches) and legs than the 1890 girl of E. L. Doctorow's *Ragtime*. But thanks to a bigger bust (33.9 inches) and torso, her figure looked better proportioned than granny's when she was a girl. Obviously a ninety-seven-pound weakling couldn't handle a woman like that on Muscle Beach, so Charles Atlas stepped into my life.

Atlas's secret was "dynamic tension," which he shared in seven languages with Tommy Grisham and 69,999 other punks around the world. Mahatma Gandhi almost became a devotee. Two years before, Atlas had expressed pity and concern for Gandhi's frail body, to which the holy man had replied: "I've met some inventive Americans, but Atlas takes the prize. Mind you, I would be delighted to have him work on me, if I could find someone to pay his passage to India."

Tommy never understood why Gandhi didn't take the course by mail, because it sure worked for Grisham. For thirty-five dollars' credit he received weekly instruction in how to match muscle against muscle in dynamic tension. It required no equipment, just a kind of narcissistic dedication to working against yourself while standing naked and sweating before a mirror in the rear bedroom of Aunt Ida's house on Poe Avenue. Within a few months Tommy rippled when he walked. He looked like Joe Palooka. The marines took him.

I was considerably younger, twelve at the time, but I, too, took up dynamic tension as well as the guitar and yodeling. For almost three years the soldiers had had the limelight. Now, it seemed to me, singers were coming on strong. Jimmie Davis, that hillbilly bard, had been elected governor of Louisiana, and up in Manhattan that skinny little crooner Frank Sinatra had to be rescued by police from a mob of thirty thousand bobby-soxers.

Besides, the war was winding down. In the Pacific the U.S. fleet dealt crippling blows to the Japanese navy, while our soldiers and marines leapfrogged from one Japanese-held island to another. The Germans, who in the preceding years had over-run Poland, Denmark, Norway, France, the Low Countries, the Balkans, North Africa, and much of Russia, were on the defensive. But the most crucial battle, the liberation of Europe, was yet to begin.

Here at home we were in a political stew. FDR was in questionable health and losing his touch with Congress, and the big question was whether he would seek a fourth term. Young, slick Tom Dewey tried his best to retire the old New Dealer, but FDR, of course, went on to victory.

By the following spring, however, FDR was dead, and Harry S Truman was our man in mid-stream, and he was a question mark. What was it that Dewey's running mate, what's-his-name, John Bricker, had said about Harry? "Harry who?"

It was the last spring of our innocence.

In '44 Elizabeth Taylor was twelve years old and in love with horses.

In '45 she was kissing Robert Taylor.

It would never be the same. We changed in 1945. My voice broke. I quit singing soprano solos in church and began to wonder and worry about girls and pimples. We lost old FDR—the passing of the father, so to speak. Oh, we won the war. But at a great cost. We would never enjoy war again. It was the year of the bomb. The year of DDT and penicillin. The year of the ballpoint pen, the year Harvard and IBM brought out the computer.

It was the year Ida Ballard died on Poe Avenue in Dallas. It was the year four marines from Ennis died on Iwo Jima. They never got together on Iwo, Joe and Airdale and Dooney and, yes, Jack. They were each there, but they never saw one another, never knew they were so close. In the thirty-seven-day siege of the island 5,931 marines died killing 19,800 Japanese. All this carnage on an island of only about eight square miles.

A sniper got Joe Crow on the second day of battle, February 20, 1945.

Sixteen days later a land mine blew off the legs of Jack Lummus. "Jack didn't live very long," his commanding officer wrote home. "I saw him soon after he was hit. With calmness and serenity, he said, 'Well, the New York Giants have lost a good man.'"

Airdale got it from a sniper the very next day.

And four days after that, Dooney died in action.

After Aunt Ida died, we never heard from Tommy. Maybe he was killed in the war and maybe he wasn't. After thirty-two years I still wonder where he is. If he's still alive I hope that he read in the papers a couple of years ago about the death of Charles Atlas. Old Atlas lasted until he was almost eighty, time enough for his dynamic tension to be recognized scientifically and to be called by another name: isometrics. But what I liked best about him was the revelation that he was not Greek at all but in the beginning Angelo Sicilano, a skinny immigrant kid from Italy who used to hang around Coney Island and wish he was as beautiful as a chalk statue of Atlas he saw in a shooting gallery.

And what I liked second best was that Angelo Sicilano, alias Charles Atlas, left, upon his death, a son named Hercules and a daughter named Diana. Diana, of course, was the goddess of the hunt. I don't know what Diana Atlas does, but Hercules Atlas teaches math in Santa Monica.

Dallas, 1976

The Christian and the Pagan

Indians are no different from white people when the preacher comes calling in the middle of supper, and the Lewises could not hide their discomfort. As their fried potatoes grew cold, they swallowed their inclination to go on with the meal and hung there in a slack-jawed and grudging gesture of hospitality. The hot little room was heavy with his intrusion, and the Reverend Bertram E. Bobb sensed it. But he would not be deterred. He was a big, beefy Choctaw, as resolute in his Christian mission as only a fundamentalist can be, and he went on talking to them in that way that preachers do in the living rooms of backsliders.

"Charles," he said to the man of the house, "Now I want you to come join us, you hear? We need you and you need us. Lots of fellowship, for you and the wife and baby." He smiled benignly at the little Apache girl in the crib.

Charles was miserable. He sweated through his T-shirt and fogged his glasses. He was embarrassed because his wife lay lacerated and bandaged on the couch, a testament to the meanness and violence that came over him whenever he stumbled home drunk. He knew the preacher knew why she had been in the hospital, and Charles had a sinking feeling that this Christian witch doctor was on to him, that Bobb and his missionaries would hound him mercilessly until he had no choice but to fall into sobriety and salvation. When the preacher finally left, leaving his card, Charles closed the door with a shudder.

"A little reluctance there," Brother Bobb said to his companion, "but he'll come around."

Rev. Bobb's friend, his right-hand man, he often said, was

Richard Soontay, a Kiowa-Apache. Richard was a mild-mannered Christian man with a Creek wife and four kids. This had not always been so. Before he met Rev. Bobb, Richard had done his share of boozing down on The Corner. A sad place, The Corner. A clutter of shabby bars at North Peak and Bryan streets where red men drank themselves into oblivion.

There are more Indians in Dallas than Custer met at Little Bighorn, and they have been streaming in off the reservations of the Southwest for the past thirteen years. The government sends them to trade schools here in the hope that they will become productive members of the American mainstream. And so most of them have. They have tended to settle in and around Oak Cliff, Casa Linda, and Garland.

For many of them, however, the move into the city is a wrenching experience. This is especially true of the tribes from the desert states. Out there on the isolated mesas they have kept much of their Indianness in spite of government schools and Christian missions, and the life they encounter in Dallas is alien to them. Tenacious in the old tongue and in the old ways, harboring some deep racial memories of their near genocide at the hands of the white man, they come here reluctantly, and some continue to live here in a bitter self-destructiveness that finds expression in the beer joints along The Corner.

It is a challenge for any preacher, and for an Indian like Rev. Bobb, The Corner is an irresistible hunting ground for sinners. He found a song leader there in the Kiowa-Apache, Richard Soontay, and now he was on the Christian warpath again, searching for lost souls with which to fill his little Open Door Bible Church in Oak Cliff. He and Soontay had handed out cards on The Corner that morning, and now at noon they were going from door to door on Annex Street, a row of apartments a few blocks from The Corner where most of the Indians new to Dallas live. The mailboxes in the lobbies show the cultural schizophrenia of these aboriginal Americans: Phillip Bluebird, C. Eagle Road, Jerimiah Joe, Noreen Two Crow—anglicized versions of Indian names which have passed into the obscurity that is the fate of oral traditions.

They came to the door of Chavez LeValdo, a Navajo-Acoma with the name of his people's Spanish conquerors. LeValdo asked them in. He was a slender young man, modishly dressed in flared pants and a beaded belt. His hair, silky and black, fell below his shoulders. He wore a headband and a stony expression on his high-boned face. He listened patiently to the Choctaw preacher and his Kiowa-Apache sidekick, and then when they were through with their pitch he asked them some questions and expressed his own religious beliefs, which to Rev. Bobb harked of paganism. The preacher had run into this before with Indians, and it always stimulated him to work harder at spreading the gospel. He tried to get a commitment from LeValdo to attend one of his services, and failing that, he urged the young man to listen to his Christian Indian radio broadcast on KSKY.

Rev. Bobb left feeling that LeValdo was beyond the pale and would probably remain so.

Bertram Bobb was a single-minded savior of men, but sometimes he had to admit that the devil had gotten there first and had done his damage to some poor souls, rendering them beyond redemption. One had to take these losses in stride. The way of the righteous was straight and narrow, and many fell by the wayside. Bobb himself had always seen the way very plainly, thanks to his parents. They had been Methodist missionaries among the Choctaws. Bobb had begun his own ministry in the Methodist church, but he had left it because of the liberal theology he thought it had begun promoting. He was now an independent preacher, connected with no church but his own out in Oak Cliff, and he saw his mission as that of meeting the spiritual needs of the growing Indian population in Dallas.

He had been fairly successful, if he did say so himself. He could count twelve tribes on the membership roll of his church. The preaching and praying was in English because none of the tribes could understand one another in Indian. Indians, from tribe to tribe, were as different as white men from nation to nation. Well, that was not entirely true, Bobb was fond of pointing out; the Choctaws, Chickasaws, Creeks, and Seminoles could

converse fairly well among themselves. But when they sang in
Rev. Bobb's church, they often sang in Indian, first one tribe's
tongue and then another's. Many of the hymns they sang were
first sung on the Trail of Tears in the 1830's, when thousands
of Indians died as they were forced to march to the new reservations in Oklahoma. The songs had what the Indians called a
mourning sound.

Still, Rev. Bobb lamented, Christian work among American
Indians was very slow. And often it was of the wrong kind. He
believed in the literal truth of the Bible, and he felt that too
many of the denominations were getting away from The Word.
The shame of it, he thought, was that the basic religious nature
of the Indian was being wasted on paganism. Its hold was still
strong on the Indian: young Chavez LeValdo was an example.
Bobb couldn't help but like LeValdo. The boy had a good mind.
He wondered if LeValdo was on peyote. He sighed and went
on about his business.

And then one Sunday he looked up from his pulpit to see
Chavez LeValdo in the congregation. It was true LeValdo sat
on the very last row, next to the door, and that there was about
him an air of subtle defiance—he wore dark sunglasses and his
arms were sternly folded—but nonetheless he was present, pre-
sumably to listen with an open mind.

Even in a congregation which was mostly Indian, LeValdo
stood out because of his long hair and headband. There were
others there just as Indian in their blood—Creek, Cherokee,
Chickasaw, and Comanche, Cheyenne and Sioux and Semi-
nole—but not so Indian, perhaps, in their dress or attitude.

Rev. Bobb made note of LeValdo to the congregation.
Every face turned to the young man. He sat there awkwardly
for a moment and then rose hesitantly to his feet to acknowledge
the introduction.

The singing began. Good old fundamentalist hymns. "Come
Thou Fount," first in English and then in Choctaw.

The song "He Hideth My Soul" said it all for Rev. Bobb.
It was his reason for being, and he saw no conflict between
being both a Choctaw and a Christian.

He hideth my soul
In the cleft of a rock
That shadows a dry thirsty land;

He hideth my life
In the depths of his love
And covers me there with his hand.

He sang his love for Christ in English, and now he sang it in Choctaw.

And then he prayed it and preached it.

But Chavez LeValdo was unmoved.

This was the second time the young man had ever sat in on a Protestant service, and he felt the same disappointment as he had before. The word *sacred* came to mind. Sacredness was what was missing here, it seemed to him. LeValdo had been taught, as a child, in a Catholic school on the reservation at Shiprock, New Mexico, and although he was now wrestling with himself over Catholicism—more and more he felt himself being drawn to the faith of his Acoma forefathers—he still liked the mystic feeling and formality of the Roman church. There was a magic, an otherworldliness in the rites of the Catholics and the Acomas that was missing in this plain little church next to the Central Expressway.

He did not question Rev. Bobb's sincerity, but what he regretted in this Choctaw Christian preacher was his Anglo-Saxon informality, his rather pedestrian and matter-of-fact approach to the spiritual. A "Rally Day" banner hung above the pulpit. Bobb could have been a well-fed coach speaking to the quarterback club or a program chairman at a Rotary luncheon. As LeValdo left the church, shaking the preacher's hand at the door, the only generous thing he could say was that he liked the Choctaw hymns although he could not understand the words.

And yet there were similarities between LeValdo and Rev. Bobb. They were both brown-skinned aboriginal Americans, both had been raised in Indian communities—Bobb in Oklahoma, LeValdo in New Mexico—both had attended Christian schools in their youth, and both had served in the U.S. Navy—

Bobb during World War II and LeValdo aboard an aircraft carrier off Vietnam.

The difference between them, perhaps, was that out in the desert of LeValdo's youth the memory of the ancients was stronger and more binding than it was in Rev. Bobb's Oklahoma. It was a fact that the Choctaws—Bobb's tribe—were one of the Five Civilized Tribes, so called by the white man because they had more easily adapted to the white man's ways than had other Indians. On the other hand, the Navajo and the Acoma—whose blood and heritage LeValdo carried—had been among the last to capitulate to the white man. High up in the hot cliffs of the Acoma, LeValdo knew that Catholicism was a white man's medicine which had not entirely replaced the notions and potions of Pueblo prophets.

The old prayers and practices yet remained, the externals of a spirit pervasive after four hundred years of excommunication. It was true that LeValdo would have his baby daughter baptized by a Catholic priest, but it was also true that he fancied himself being buried, when his time came, in the Indian way with his moccasins and war paint on. The ways of his ancestors rose up in him and made him reluctant to cut his hair, and they worked in him when he carved dolls and made drums and shields of rawhide.

Chavez LeValdo did not consider himself a throwback to the past. There was enough of the white man's influence in him to cause him to count time and to measure it by the Newtonian dimensions of past, present, and future. And he saw himself as being in tune with these three references, like the *paisano* bird which was painted on Indian drums. The *paisano* had four toes on each foot. Two pointed to the back, the past, and two pointed to the front, the future. The leg itself came right down upon the ground of the present. And here was LeValdo himself, living in the urban clot of modern Dallas, taking advantage of a government grant which allowed him to learn how to repair and maintain a computer. He spoke six languages: Navajo, Acoma, English, Fortran, Cobol, and Compass—the last three being computer idiom.

Pagan? Peyote?

Well he had never tasted the cactus bud, and he had never understood why white men called the faith of his forefathers pagan. The Old Man of the Sky was the husband of the Old Woman of the Earth, and all things came from their union, just as Raquel came from Chavez's union with his wife Eunice. Mankind and the animals, the earth and the sky with their elements, all had the same kind of life. And a person had to be in harmony with the life in all things. The way was in religion, in a prayerful reverence for every stick and stone and bird and flower and brother. It was beautiful, he thought.

Chavez LeValdo went home to his apartment and got out his *kethawn* box. It had been given him by one of the elders of his tribe, an old Navajo who had taught him the ancient chants. It was a case made of cloth, and in it were prayer sticks and talismans of his people's sacred rites. He burned a stick and rubbed soot on his face and sang the magic chants that were said to ward off evil influences. Now he felt clean again and strong enough to cope with the white man's world. He was also hungry. He went into the kitchen and made a peanut butter sandwich.

Dallas, 1972

H. L. Hunt's Long Good-bye

That last weekend in November was almost too much, even for astrologers and students of the absurd. It began predictably enough—former President Nixon was too ill to testify at the Watergate cover-up trial, doctors had decided—but then strange headlines began to pop out. Popular Princess Elizabeth Bagaya, the foreign minister of Uganda, was dismissed by President Idi Amin after he charged that she had made love to a European in the restroom of the Orly Airport in Paris. In Philadelphia, family pressure and the delicate political position of Vice-President-designate Nelson Rockefeller forced Happy Rockefeller's seventy-seven-year-old millionaire aunt, Rachel Fitler, to call off her engagement to Michael Wilson, her twenty-nine-year-old chauffeur. In our other staid, conservative, old-line town, Harvard students were giving standing ovations to none other than Fanne Fox, the Tidal Basin Bombshell who had stripped Congressman Wilbur Mills of his doughty dignity and made of him a dirty old man.

It was a seductive, if lurid, time to be alive, and every health faddist knew that H. L. Hunt was trying. At eighty-five he was munching dates and doing the full lotus and aiming at a century and more. But then secretly, before only family and friends, he began to fail. And on that last Friday in November he died in Dallas' Baylor University Medical Center of pneumonia and complications from cancer. The weekend was yet full of surprises. The Bears of Baylor University, some of Hunt's fellow Baptists, were outscoring the Rice University football team to cap off their first conference championship in fifty years.

It would have been a fitting final balm for the world's richest Baptist and football fan.

But perhaps it is just as well that Hunt was not aware of the events that transpired on the last day of his life. For transcending everything was the news—in a surprise announcement from Secretary of State Henry Kissinger—that President Ford would visit Peking in 1975. What an irony to go down to! Haroldson Lafayette Hunt, Jr., had been notoriously stingy with his money, except in one endeavor. Like a Daddy Warbucks, he had waged a long and expensive crusade against communism and what he considered its influence here. Joe McCarthy and Douglas Mac-Arthur had been his idols. Nixon, he thought, had been a dupe for allowing Kissinger to subvert us into a rapprochement with China and Soviet Russia. Hunt's last hope lay in Gerald Ford, whom he had recommended to Nixon as a vice-president back before 1960. Yes, it was just as well.

If the highest estimates of H. L. Hunt's wealth are true, he was not only four times as rich as all the Rockefellers, but he was also nine times richer than all the accumulated wealth of all the presidents of the United States—all thirty-eight of them from George Washington to Gerald Ford. Some sheiks of Araby may scoff at that two or five billion—whatever it is—now, but if they hadn't taken the Libyan fields from him two years ago, he'd still be the richest man in the world. I'm not hung up on his money, though. What I liked about old H. L. was the originality and richness of his character.

The big rich are not always fascinating, but Hunt was. Take *Fortune* magazine's head count on the new centimillion-aires in America. The Yellow Pages make better reading. Once it was at least vulgar to have suddenly made a fortune. Now it's just dull. Can you imagine squeezing oranges for a living? That's what Anthony Rossi does down in Florida, and in the last six years it has made him seventy million dollars. He's one of thirty-nine men in the country *Fortune* says has made at least fifty million dollars since 1968. The list doesn't include people who have inherited that much or who made it before 1968, so it's an interesting insight into our newest crop of Croesuses. What emerges is not a saga of flamboyant wheeling and dealing, but instead a parade of pedestrian types who have cornered the market on faucets and tire treads, of people who purvey pet foods and discount clothing. I didn't see a sugar daddy among them. If they throw their money away, it is not to blondes but to Baptist churches and Bible colleges.

But H. L., now, he was many men in one, multitudinous and contradictory. Good and bad, but on a larger scale, right out of Ayn Rand. In an age of midgets and conformists he was a rogue who broke rules and cut a large swath and then, at last, lay down with a smile and allowed the ubiquitous and unctuous preachers to make of him a monument to nobility. He knew they would, because he knew human nature. The will, after all, was still to be read. If ever a dead man looked satisfied with himself, at peace and in repose and yet somehow expectant, it was Mr. Hunt.

He lay in an open casket at First Baptist, the world's largest and richest Baptist church. The church, a mighty fortress covering several downtown blocks in Dallas, is noted as a rock against theological and social heresy. Only recently has the congregation, which numbers twenty thousand, been moved to accept a Negro member. Hunt was not necessarily the most famous member of First Baptist; Billy Graham is one, too, though he was not at the funeral. The presiding preacher was the pastor, Dr. W. A. Criswell, a compelling and charismatic fundamentalist who helped convert Hunt after his second marriage seventeen years ago. That was a conversion to match Saul's when he became Paul. Perhaps a more profane comparison would be the transfiguration of that old rip-roaring, foulmouthed drunk, Sam Houston. It was a woman that helped old Sam see the light: his second wife, the resourceful and enduring Margaret Lea. Legend has it that H. L. was equally rollicking, and history knows that Ruth Ray Wright brought him to heel in a chorus of hallelujahs.

Ruth was a Hunt Oil secretary H. L. married in 1957, two years after the death of his first wife, Lyda Bunker. The second marriage, when Hunt was sixty-eight, confronted the six children of his first bed—Lamar, Nelson Bunker, W. Herbert, H. L. III, Margaret, and Caroline—with a stepmother thirty years younger than their father. They also faced four sibling rivals in the children of Ruth: Ray Lee, June, Helen, and Swanee, the issue of "a former marriage." After Hunt formally adopted them, Ruth revealed that Hunt was, indeed, their true father. Ruth, a pretty blonde with Southern belle manners, seemed just the right tonic for the old rascal. It wasn't long before she and the preacher put the Lord on H. L., turned him away from gambling and cigars, and led him down the aisle to salvation. Dr. Criswell baptized Hunt and his new family—and from then on they were all devout in the faith.

In his last years Hunt was a doting family man, a molting old lion in winter. He loved to lay up there in his outsized replica of Mount Vernon and sing hymns with Ruth and the youngest girls. As he began to fail, there was one song he could not bear to hear: "Swing Low, Sweet Chariot," where it keeps repeating, "comin' for to carry me home. . . ."

It was my first time to hear Brother Criswell preach, and I waited expectantly as the pews filled. People quietly streamed in, filling up the benches except for a few in the balcony. It was more like a theater than a church. There were even little traffic signs and admonitions. I dutifully took note that "In Case of Emergency," I was to "Please Use Exit 2." Another said, "Please Be Reverent." Tommy Brinkley, the organist, began to play. First, "The Solid Rock," and then, "This Is My Country." Every now and then a knot of mourners would get up from their seats and go gaze at the body. Mr. Hunt was laid out in a dark, pin-striped suit. He was a beautiful man, his pink and fine, bold head more delicately carved than pictures had portrayed. He was thinner than I had thought, his nose an aristocratic legacy of his Huguenot forebears. Others had compared him in the flesh to Herbert Hoover, but I saw in him a Leopold Stokowski. He was a genius, in a way, an entrepreneur, an impresario, a maestro of money. Most of us pass through town unnoticed. He made ripples, made men note his passing. He had made his mark, like the conquistador of old who, traveling

in the wilderness of New Mexico, had inscribed upon the rock,
"Pasó por Aquí."

The day before the funeral I had walked to the Kentucky
Fried Chicken stand and had ordered a box of B, regular recipe,
and an iced Coke. They were selling copies of Colonel Harland
Sanders's autobiography, so I bought one. My mind was on Hunt
and his death, and it struck me, in an amusing way, that he and
the old bird cook shared some similarities. The colonel called
his book *Life As I Have Known It Has Been FINGER LICKIN'
GOOD*, and inside the jacket was a rundown of the colonel's
checkered career. Sixth-grade dropout, farmhand at age twelve,
army mule tender, locomotive fireman, railroad section hand,
aspiring lawyer, insurance salesman, ferryboat entrepreneur,
chamber of commerce secretary, tire salesman, amateur obste-
trician, unsuccessful political candidate, gas station dealer, motel
operator, restaurateur, until finally, at the age of sixty-five, a new
interstate highway snatched the traffic away from his corner,
leaving the colonel with nothing but a Social Security check and
a secret recipe for fried chicken. Dad-gummit! The colonel was
seventy-four before someone paid him two million dollars for
his fried chicken franchise. He went on to get religion and sue
the people who bought him out something like twenty-two
times, for various and sticky reasons.

Sitting there licking my fingers, I decided to outline Hunt's
career the way the colonel had his. This is what I came up with,
and it probably isn't complete: never went to school, farmhand
till fifteen, freight train and flophouse hobo, dishwasher, cowboy, lumberjack, laborer, sheepherder, carpenter, mule team
driver, cardsharp gambler, cotton planter, oil lease hound, oil
operator, big-time gambler, farmer, rancher, real estate man,
food processor, manufacturer, author, philosopher, political
propagandist, unsuccessful advisor to four presidents, and, of
course, at one time or another the world's richest man. Compared to Hunt, the colonel is chicken feed.

Hunt's life was highly American—as bodacious and ungoverned as the age that made him. He was born and raised on
a five-hundred-acre farm near Ramsey, Illinois, the youngest of

eight children in a well-to-do family. The early years of his youth were among the most prosperous in American history, as the great captains of industry followed the pioneers' movement to the west. There was the Panic of 1893, when Hunt was four and Grover Cleveland was president, and it grew into our first serious depression, but that soon was dispelled by a resurgence of production and patriotism—the latter culminating in Teddy Roosevelt's charge up San Juan Hill. The Roughrider was Hunt's hero; when Roosevelt tried to make a comeback in 1912 as the "old Bull Moose," Hunt, then twenty-three and running a cotton plantation down in Mississippi, rode all the way back to Illinois to vote for Roosevelt for president. Hunt himself seemed to imitate, throughout his long life, the vim and vigor of the president.

The Land Panic of 1921 destroyed his cotton venture, and Hunt moved on to El Dorado, Arkansas. Oil had been found, and the town was booming. Old-timers claim H. L. came to town as a gambler and won his first oil well in a game of five-card stud. Hunt admitted he was something of a hustler, but he insisted that he had gotten his stake by shrewdly trading leases. From El Dorado he moved to Smackover in Arkansas, Urania in Louisiana, and out to West Texas—anywhere there was the smell of oil and a sucker at a card table.

As his luck held, Hunt began to form a political philosophy to match his new fortune. Where once he had admired a strong man in the White House, such as Teddy Roosevelt, now he came to value weak men at the helm of government. Young Hunt was not alone. The 1920's were an era of giants in every endeavor except the presidency. There were great heroes in sports—men such as Dempsey and Cobb and Ruth, Thorpe and Red Grange—but as president there was a congenital weakling, a bag of wind named Warren G. Harding. There was Man o' War on the racetrack, Lucky Lindy in the sky, George Gershwin on the radio, Mary Pickford on the silver screen, and in the White House that old corpse Calvin Coolidge. And H. L. Hunt loved him. By the end of the decade, when the country was going from riches to rags, Herbert Hoover was in the White House, a rags-to-riches man. It was all caterwampus. But not for Hunt, because out in the dogwood and deep red clay of East Texas there was a fortune to be made.

H. L. Hunt was already a millionaire, when, at the height of the panic in 1930, he bought out Dad Joiner's strike in East Texas. Joiner had drilled with money raised among the poor farmers of the area, but by the time he had brought the first few wells in, he found that the depression had created an oil glut, and he couldn't sell his leases to the majors because of some clouded titles. But Hunt didn't lay back. For $50,000 in cash, $45,000 in notes, and a guarantee of $1.3 million from future production, he took over a field that turned out to tap a lake of oil forty-three miles long and up to nine miles wide. Hunt's share of the profits came to $100 million, at least. By 1940 H. L. was a billionaire and expanding into the Middle East. During World War II he produced more oil, here and abroad, than did Germany, Italy, and Japan. By 1960 he was the world's richest man. By that time, his old partner in East Texas, Columbus Marvin ("Dad") Joiner, had been broken and buried thirteen years.

A murmur arose from the congregation. A small black man, who seemed to materialize from nowhere, stood before the coffin and drew a sword. He waved it before the dead man, sheathed it, and exited by a side door. It seemed an act of defiance, and I—and I'm sure others—thought, my God, is he some revolutionary, some Symbionese Liberationist come to defame the dead capitalist's memory? Later the mysterious man identified himself as Louis Lyons, a forty-four-year-old ex-convict Hunt had befriended. He had come to salute the old Caesar, not to damn him.

The family had not yet entered the sanctuary, but at our backs we were startled to see an unmistakable likeness of the dead man standing in the doorway. It could have been Hunt himself, thirty years younger. "Hassie!" someone whispered. And indeed it was. Haroldson Lafayette Hunt III, the old man's eldest son, the gentle one who was said to live in a world all his own. Some great tragedy had befallen him, and he had lived close to the side of his father. Once, it was said, he had shown the same managerial genius as the father, only to retreat from the world of men and affairs. Some said Hassie's tragedy was his experience in the Second World War. Others said he had never gone to war, that he had changed because he could not stand up to the pressure of being a great man's son. Is it indelicate and inaccurate of me to slip here into hearsay? What the mourners said that day, and what the press and other people wrote and said, were the stuff of the Hunt legend. For a man so prominent yet so private, this legend is what lives on, just as it bathes the children in the same light. In a moment Brother Criswell himself would be myth-making, and I would listen to that. Right now I watched Hassie Hunt. He walked down the aisle, looked at his dead father, and wept. Then he returned to his post behind us, near the door. There was in him a sad dignity.

The organist launched into "God Bless America," the cue for Brother Criswell, followed by the family, to enter the stage. The casket was closed. The family sat to the left down front, and Brother Criswell stood at the pulpit above the casket. He is in his sixties, a silver-haired, handsome man with a large head and a lantern jaw. Many of his congregation drive great distances—past closer Baptist churches—to hear him preach. His Wednesday night prayer meetings had to be moved from a hall seating seven hundred into the main auditorium to handle the crowd. On Sundays the crush is like a small Cotton Bowl. Worshipers often have to stand. Parking lot attendants with walkie-talkies are all about the grounds. Criswell has written at least a dozen books, the most recent entitled *Why I Believe in the Literal Word of the Bible.* The literal fact of First Baptist is extraordinary, approaching legend. Housed in a complex which includes an eleven-story office building, First Baptist Church is a publishing house; a television and recording studio which broadcasts Sunday services; a credit union; and a country club and health spa which includes gymnasiums, bowling lanes, a skating rink, and snack bars; as well as, of course, the church school and the church itself. First Baptist has twenty-two choirs, one of which travels throughout the world. The pastor's wife plays saxophone in the church's swing band, and H. L. Hunt's third daughter, June, used to sing solo in one of the choirs before she went to Nashville to record and tour with her gospel singing engagements.

June Hunt would sing, Brother Criswell announced, a song that her father loved so well. It was about Jesus. "I shall know him," it went, "by the print of the nails in his hand." June is a tall, good-looking blonde, and she sang with poise and warmth, clear-eyed and smiling without a break in her voice. Brother Criswell read scripture. "Great and noble father," he intoned, "teach us to number our days. . . . The grass withereth, the flower fadeth. . . ."

H. L. Hunt knew only too well that grass withereth, but he tried to forestall the aging process as long as he could. He developed a keen interest in what enabled other men to live beyond the usual life span. When items appeared in the newspapers about some Methuselah holding forth in some far corner of the world, Hunt would have his secretary call the Associated Press, or even the character in question, to see if there might be more details he could pick up.

In September, 1972, Rena Pederson of the *Dallas Morning News* went to the Hunt home to interview him at breakfast. Hunt sat munching grapes, pecans, dates, and apricots. He also had before him an array of fruit juices and bouillon. All of a sudden he dropped to the floor on all fours and began crawling about. "I'm a crank about creeping!" he cried, rounding the antique dining table on his hands and knees.

"Don't go too fast," Mrs. Hunt cautioned.

"Yes, please slow down," the *News* photographer begged. "I want to get your picture."

"They never can keep up with me," he cackled, returning to the table. "Yahoo!" he whooped, and ordered a date for everyone. He bit into a pecan and declared, "I used to be the world's Number One softshell pecan grower. I suppose I still am. I eat them instead of meat."

To reporter Pederson's amazement, the billionaire barraged her with health food information. Avoid white bread and white sugar. He recommended his own bread of cracked wheat and honey. He grew most of his own vegetables in a three-acre garden at the side of the mansion and ate them as raw as possible and salt-free. He handed her literature: pamphlets on health, a mimeographed Bible verse, and an article he had written about the benefits of creeping.

"I have lots of money," he laughed, "so they call me the 'Billionaire Health Crank.' Heh Heh Heh."

At that time Hunt was convinced he had a good chance to live as long as the world record holder, a Russian the Soviets claim was 167. He liked to compare himself to the Hunzakuts of the Himalayas, who played polo into their hundredth year.

Frank Tolbert, the *Dallas Morning News* columnist and author, once put Hunt onto buying a Mexican border ranch because of the curative power of its springs. Tolbert claims to be the first writer Hunt ever consented to see. This was back in 1948, when Hunt was as reclusive as Howard Hughes. Tolbert didn't do too badly by him, so Hunt trusted him and was open to most of the other journalists who began beating a path to his door. Anyway, one day Hunt got all excited over Tolbert's tales about an old resort ranch at Indian Hot Springs on the Rio Grande about 125 miles downstream from El Paso. There was a spring on the place called Geronimo Springs, which the old-timers out there likened to a fountain of youth. It revived an old feller's interest in sex and exorcised sores and such. The Vanderbilts once used it as a spa, and Pancho Villa used to dip in it to rid himself of gonorrhea. Hunt bought the retreat, and you rarely saw him without his old leather valise, which contained bottled mineral water from its healing springs. Along with the water he usually had some of his bread, made of wheat from the Panhandle soil of Deaf Smith County.

One summer day a few years back Hunt showed up in Judge Tom Neely's general store out at Sierra Blanca, near Fort Bliss. He had just returned from his hot springs, so he passed his water bottle and bread to the men about and joined them in a game of checkers, at which he was mightily skilled. Judge Neely, who is the Roy Bean of Hudspeth County, was complaining about a foot ailment, when to his surprise the world's richest man got up from the checkerboard and got down on his knees and pulled off Neely's boots and socks. "He started rubbing my feet," the judge said. "At first I felt bad about it, a man like that on his knees rubbing my old feet, but then I felt good about it, and it did make me feel a lot better."

Dr. James Draper, the young associate pastor, followed Dr. Criswell. He said a prayer for Hunt and his survivors and then, to my astonishment, called (in what I thought was a very pointed way) for some of the Hunts who had not accepted Christ to do so. I know that preachers grab you when they can get your attention, but at your father's funeral? He was obviously aiming at someone among the older children, all of whom are grown and quite competent to come to God in their own fashion. It didn't help matters much when he extended the invitation to the rest of us who might be beyond the fold.

Dr. Criswell came back to announce that the last hymn that H. L. Hunt had heard was one that had been broadcast on television a Sunday or so before, and that Beverly Terrell, a close friend of the Hunts, was going to sing it. She dedicated the song not to a man who was wealthy, but to the God who made the wealth of this world. "Voices of a million angels," she sang, "could not express my gratitude. . . . All that I am and ever hope to be . . . I owe it all to thee, God. . . ."

Sidney Latham, Hunt's long-time friend and personal attorney, a retired vice-president of Hunt Oil Company, delivered the eulogy. He described Hunt as one of the finest Christians he had ever known. Hunt's faith was, he said, in keeping with the faith and nobility of the company and of the family who founded it.

He said something I liked. "Hunt," he said, "moved in and about the timberlines of life where the timid fear to venture." Sure, Latham said, Hunt had his faults. He was all too human, the old lawyer proposed, and certainly, he added, Hunt was one of the most misunderstood men who ever drew public comment. He described his old colleague as a patriot who proved that the American way would work, but that in all candor, after all the millions were made, signed, sealed, and delivered, the greatest happiness Hunt had had was the Sunday night he joined the church. "He said it was the best and biggest trade he had ever made," Latham said, raising his voice. "He said he had traded the here for the hereafter, and he was pleased."

What did Hunt have here? Certainly America's largest private fortune. And, some said, a divided family fighting over it —the children of the dead wife versus the children of the living wife. There were signs of struggle even before the old man's death, hidden beneath a confusing tangle of lawsuits and investigations, both private and public, that involved not only the Hunts and their employees but, of all things, Watergate-ridden Richard Nixon, his attorney general, John Connally, Senator James Eastland, Israel's Golda Meir, and the Arab terrorists Al Fatah.

The intrigue surfaced routinely enough four years ago when a suburban Dallas policeman stopped Jon Joseph Kelly for running a stop sign. Kelly, a twenty-five-year-old Houston man, identified himself as a private detective. The patrolman noticed a tape recorder in Kelly's back seat. "When I asked him if he was working on a divorce case," the policeman later recalled, "he stepped on the gas and took off. If he hadn't panicked, I wouldn't have hauled him in, and none of this would have come out."

What came out was this: The FBI discovered that Kelly and a sidekick, Patrick McCann, had placed wiretaps in the homes of four Hunt Oil executives, among them Paul Rothermel, H. L. Hunt's chief security man. Rothermel, a former FBI man and an attorney, claimed that in 1969 he had persuaded Hunt to change his will to the greater benefit of the second Mrs. Hunt and her children. Since then, odd things had been happening, and Rothermel believed that the older Hunt sons were behind them. Kelly and McCann, however, remained mute —until they got three years in prison. Then they fingered two of the older Hunt sons, Nelson Bunker and W. Herbert Hunt, as the plotters and paymasters. Nelson and Herbert were indicted on wiretapping charges, but only after a curiously long time lag. They have since admitted that they ordered "legal investigations" of Rothermel and the other executives, but not wiretaps. They contend their motive was not to spy on their father's

will making, but to trace millions of dollars which were alleg-
edly siphoned off into dummy companies. They backed up their
charges with a suit against Rothermel and two other company
officials. Since then, Kelly has sued Nelson and W. Herbert
Hunt, complaining that they ruined his reputation and career.
The Rothermels have retaliated with a suit against the Hunts,
Mrs. Rothermel claiming that the operatives interfered with her
work as a psychiatrist's aide by eavesdropping on her patients.

That's the private war.

Publicly, three federal grand juries have returned indictments against nine men, including the two Hunt boys. Mean-
while, for almost a year a fourth federal grand jury in Dallas has
been investigating the three-year time lag in getting the wiretap
indictments against the Hunt brothers. Hunt sources allege that
President Nixon and his men promised Nelson Bunker and his
brother immunity from prosecution if the Hunts would give
the FBI a list of Al Fatah agents in the United States. Nelson
Bunker, because of his attempts to keep Hunt oil fields from
being nationalized by Libya, felt himself a target for assassina-
tion and therefore kept a close count of Al Fatah agents in this
country. Nelson Bunker and his father met President Nixon at
the celebrated barbecue at John Connally's Floresville ranch in
the autumn of 1972. Soon after, Nelson Bunker huddled with
Richard Kleindienst, then the new boss of the Justice Department, at the plantation of Mississippi Senator James Eastland.
Hunt sources claim that Nelson Bunker came through for the
FBI and that the information helped foil a plot against Golda
Meir when she visited New York in March, 1973. The indictments against Nelson Bunker and his brother went through
anyway. In April, Kleindienst fell to Watergate. The next
month Libya's Colonel Qadhafi confiscated the Hunt holdings
in the Sahara desert.

Eventually a jury would find the two Hunt brothers innocent of wiretapping, but for a while there Nelson Bunker Hunt
is said to have felt betrayed, and that's putting it mildly. At
one time Libya was his happy hunting ground. He negotiated
Hunt Oil's vast holdings there, wined and dined the inaugura-

tion of the new empire, and had high friends all over the Arab World. But because of his country's friendship toward Israel and their own growing nationalism, the Arabs turned against him. Nixon let him down. And then, two days after the burial of his father, he learned that the old man had bequeathed him a stunner. The will gave Mrs. Hunt 100 percent of the patriarch's stock in Hunt Oil, distributing to Nelson Bunker and the other nine children and their families the rest of the estate. True to his fashion, the old man kept it all in the family, with Ruth's offspring seemingly getting the upper hand. Ray Hunt, the oldest son of the second set, was named as sole executor. And to insure compliance, H. L. stipulated that any beneficiary who challenged the will in any way would be cut off without a cent. That did not happen. Indeed, both sides of the family seemed to come together in mutual interest.

Few godfathers, whether Irish or Italian, political or criminal, have left progeny with such a bounty of brains and ability. Nelson Bunker is an aggressive go-getter with many of his father's talents. Politically, he is a chip off the old genus *Betula,* a Birch not for bending, and has been almost as active as H. L. in backing Robert Welch and George Wallace. In 1973 he and Herbert, who himself is no slouch at real estate development, were reported to have cornered the market on silver bullion. They are now said to be trying to do the same thing with America's beet refining. Bunker is supposed to have more racehorses than any other breeder in the country, as well as some of the best Charolais in the cattle business.

Lamar Hunt, of course, is probably better known than any of the boys because he took his father's gaming instincts and love of sport and patiently turned the losing Dallas Texans into the winning Kansas City Chiefs. Lamar and his brother-in-law, Al G. Hill, put World Championship Tennis on tour, and Lamar helped kick life into the North American Soccer League with Kyle Rote, Jr., and the Dallas Tornado. The stepbrother and fifth son, Ray Lee Hunt, the executor of the will, is showing the same savvy with his dealings in downtown Dallas. Ray is also the angel of the new magazine, *D.*

As for the five daughters, June, with her singing career, is the most visible, but the others all have done well, and each is as individual as the brothers. Margaret married Al Hill, the sportsman and banker; Caroline married Hugo Schoellkopf, scion of one of Dallas' first families; and Helen and Swanee are young women of exceptional talents, each showing a flare for the arts and humanities.

Those children, along with twenty-five grandchildren and five great-grandchildren, are the sum of H. L. Hunt as a family man and provider—his private behest.

He went public in only one way really, and that was in his products, which included his political philosophy. William F. Buckley, Jr., probably has never opened a can of HLH corn, but the old man's political gumbo he tasted and found lacking. Buckley says politics was the least of H. L. Hunt's talents, that his books were silly, and that Hunt did more harm than good to the conservative movement. In a column published shortly after Hunt's death, fellow Texan Buckley declared that Hunt had left "capitalism a bad name, not, goodness knows, by frenzies of extravagance, but by his eccentric understanding of public affairs, his yahoo bigotry and his appallingly bad manners."

Yet Hunt was hardly a conservative—at least not as that term is used in American politics—and never claimed to be. I'm not quite sure how Hunt bothered Buckley. He made me nervous all right, but in some of the same ways that Buckley does. If Hunt had had his way, Senator Joe McCarthy would have purged every "pinko" and "subversive" from the roll call of American patriotism. Douglas MacArthur would have been president instead of Dwight Eisenhower, and we would have gotten out of the United Nations long ago and bombed the bejeesus out of Russia and Red China to deter their nuclear capacity before it matched our own. Hunt in 1966 told *Playboy* magazine that the air force's General George C. Kenney had had such a plan back in 1950, and Hunt wished we had used it.

Hunt called himself a "constructive." A conservative, he argued, tended to put a weight around the neck of liberty. He defined liberty as "freedom for the individual to do whatever he likes consistent with organized society and good taste." The word *conservative*, he went on, "denotes mossback, reactionary, and old-fogeyism."

This smacks to me of classic liberalism, and I said as much on a Dallas television show a few years back. Hunt was intrigued by my calling him a liberal, and he asked for a copy of my remarks. If they offended him, it never reached me. I couched my argument in this context: the terms *liberal* and *conservative* came to be used late in the eighteenth and early nineteenth centuries out of the froth of the French Revolution and Napoleon's rise and fall. The liberal believed first of all in the independence and autonomy of the individual answering only to his conscience. A free individual, the liberal believed, had an unlimited capacity for self-development and improvement. In personal freedom, man could create on this earth near-perfect conditions. Unconstrained man, giving full play to his personality! A nice definition of H. L. Hunt. But the liberal wasn't an anarchist. One man's self-expression could not impinge on the freedom of other men, and this fits nicely into Hunt's qualifications about "organized society and good taste" in his description of a "constructive." Liberals, however, were not to be confused with democrats. Liberals came to distrust the common man because they feared his ignorance; they suspected that he could be manipulated by despots. Liberals opposed universal vote, limiting suffrage to the propertied classes. And this nicely defines *Alpaca*, Hunt's model republic. Hunt's utopia was not unlike Plato's *Republic*. If Hunt's was oligarchical and built upon mammon, Plato's was a communistic aristocracy built upon a pathological passion for order that was self-defeating.

Neither old theorist could influence anyone to take his advice. Plato thought for a while that he might persuade Dionysus II, the ruler of Syracuse, to put his ideas into actual practice, but it was an unhappy wedding of the philosopher and the king. Twenty-three hundred years later, Hunt was just as pushy with his programs to Presidents Eisenhower, Kennedy, Johnson, and Nixon; but Booth Mooney, who was Hunt's man in Washington, admitted that "it is not of record that any of them solicited the counsel so freely offered. . . ." It was Lyndon Johnson that Hunt especially liked. But as Mooney has written, "Advise as the old gentleman might, it was all of no use. Johnson never gave the slightly sign of paying any attention to the snowstorm of memoranda from Dallas, which for a time descended on the White House at the rate of four or five a week."

Other Americans did listen. For six years in the 1950's. Hunt had Dan Smoot on radio and television with "Facts Forum," a public affairs program which was finally replaced by "Life Line." Hunt saw "Life Line" as a kind of Voice of America in the heart of the heart of the country; at its peak a few years ago "Life Line" was carried by 531 radio stations and heard by an estimated five million Americans. The guiding principle of "Life Line" is anticommunism, and it is delivered in fire and brimstone sermons about the evils of everything that has transpired since Sherman rode through Georgia and Roosevelt sold out at Yalta. The sum of it seems to have given form to some of the heart of darkness and fear of change that is in us all. The foe is everywhere, subversive and conspiratorial, and the instinct is to stack rifles in the basement and vote against minorities and longhairs and the welfare state.

There is, however, one truth we should accept from H. L. Hunt without reservation: you can't *buy* friends, domestic or foreign. He knew that long before he was rich, and so he never tried. The one thing you *can* buy, most of the time, is power, even political power and even in a republic. And that, ironically, or not so ironically, H. L. Hunt did not do either. And that's the beauty of the man for me. His mouth always got in the way of his money and turned the right people off.

Hunt himself did not seem to suffer from all that hate and fear and trembling that he supported. He was altogether himself in an age of cover and cosmetics. He had more deer around Mount Vernon than dogs, and his bark was worse than his bite unless you were a radish or a ravishing woman. We forget that he was not always old and wispy-haired and hyped on greens and granola. Once you could catch him each year at the state fair, manning a modest booth displaying his HLH products and handing out a goodwill bag which contained one of his paperback books—perhaps *Alpaca*—along with a packet of "freedom talks" from "Life Line" as well as a free sample of Gastro-Magic, his special brand of relief from heartburn and indigestion.

Some have painted him as sinister, the right-wing capitalist who conveniently left town the day JFK was killed in Dallas, but I can't let my paranoia run away in that direction, either. I don't think Hunt conspired to kill the president any more than I think Nelson Rockefeller is in league with Henry Kissinger to turn us over to the communists. Which means, I guess, that I give H. L. Hunt more credit than he gave Rocky and the rest of us.

Dr. Criswell returned to his pulpit. "Worthy, noble father," he cried, his voice breaking, "sentimental about his home and children, good to them beyond compare. Especially to the child who was not well. Oh yes, I often referred to him as Mr. Golden Heart."

And on he went, describing Hunt as a man too big for one life, a man wise as Solomon. "Haroldson Lafayette Hunt, living giant with gentle touch . . . *au revoir, auf Wiedersehen*, till we meet again. . . ."

An hour later Hunt was buried, in private ceremonies, beside the grave of his first wife in Hillcrest Memorial Park in north Dallas.

Dallas, 1975

The Santa Berta

Even in the glare of day the car is insignificant, a dusty rattle making its tedious way through the country, of no account in the blaze of sky and the sweep of plain. The land is a paradox, sunlit but brooding, open but impassive, above all impersonal, and it takes no note of the movement on the road.

I and my machine, we are nothing in the primordial play of hawk and cloud and coyote and burrow. The brush, the butte, the ragged arroyo are as they were the day before and the day before that on back through the passing of the latest ranch Cadillac and the first conquistador.

Little had changed in the years since I had been a summer hand in Kenedy County. The world had turned upside down! But that was a foreign country, the rest of the world. Elsewhere in South Texas there had been rumblings. It was as if the people, after centuries of Indian torpor, had roused themselves. It was as if some bugler in the mountains was calling them to arms. The priests in San Antonio, usually the most passive of men, rebelled and got rid of their stern old archbishop. Mexican school children demonstrated in the dust for their rights, and the Texas Rangers, that outpost of Aryan authority, repented and pinned a badge on a man named Rodriquez. But here on these ranches the sun came up and the sun went down. A rain was an event.

That first time out, twenty-four years ago, I was fifteen miles out of Kingsville on U.S. 77 when my car overheated. The gas station attendant at Riviera said it was one hundred in the shade. "Where you headed?"

"Raymondville, or almost."

"Better put more than water in this buggy. There's not another gas stop for sixty miles."

"What's between here and there?"

He laughed. "I'd say nuthin' but lonesome country, a lotta rattlesnakes, and a few thirsty Mexicans."

Few was right. The population density was one person for every two square miles, but even that ratio was misleading. You could ride for miles and not see a house. Most of the county's seven hundred residents were huddled about the headquarters of the big ranches, where there was work and a modicum of amenities.

It was funny how such a simple thing as a tree tall enough to shade you became precious and worth resting under. The chaparral was a tangle of treachery. Jesús La Feria told me so, and I believed him. We had shared the umbrella of a roadside oak that July a quarter-century before—I lost and letting my car radiator cool, he trying to revive with drinking water the wilting funeral flowers that covered a casket in the back of his hearse. On the door panels of the death wagon, carved in gilded wood, was the legend:

Jesús & Jesús

Master Morticians

Mirando City, Texas

An old woman from one of the ranches of his boyhood had died, and Jesús had taken her to his establishment, seventy miles to the west, to embalm the body. Now he was returning her for burial that afternoon. An uncle, a superintendent for an oil company, had hired me to nightwatch a drilling rig going up on the Armstrong Ranch, and I, eighteen and a stranger to the border country, had lost my way on one of the back roads.

Jesús La Feria gave me excellent directions. He was a large man, his heavy body entombed in a black suit, all canopied by a big, black hat. He sank to his haunches beneath the tree, removed his sombrero, and poured the water on his steaming scalp. His neck was black as a bois d'arc root. Suddenly he reached out and swatted me, or rather a large red ant that had been crawling up my pants leg.

It startled me, and he laughed. "Better me hit you than the

hormiga," he said. "Stand still out here, and you're in trouble, my friend. Think of all the things that can get you." In spite of his warning, we sat for a while, and I listened as he described with a kind of pagan pride the predatory nature of his homeland. He was an eloquent and convincing man, and when we parted I prayed nightfall would not find me stranded.

I coaxed my boiling Buick through the badlands, mindful that humankind was miles to go. "Think of all the things that can get you." I could think of nothing else! Rattlers, scorpions, tarantulas, the wild dogs, the snorting bulls that thundered through the brush. Even the frogs grew horns. Everything flora or fauna either pricked or pounced. It was only later, in the comfort of the drilling company bunkhouse, that I could see the strange beauty of Jesús's vision.

"My people have a saying," he had said. "It is that the only thing soft and white in this country is the underbelly of lizards and women."

A later time. Another trip. I remember a squinty-eyed man with a pistol on his hip and a badge on his breast. He and his wife were the sole survivors of a place called Armstrong after the ranching family. All there was to it was a rickety house with a post office sign tacked to the porch and some cattle loading pens alongside the railroad track. The man said he was the deputy sheriff; his wife was the postmistress.

"Yep," he agreed. "This is peculiar country. The county runs 'bout fifty miles long and forty miles wide, and you can't find a grocery store, fillin' station, beer joint, or bank in it. And if you're hungry, forget it. No café, either."

Until ten years before, there had been no public highway. The eighty-mile-long expanse of beach, a few miles to the east where the Gulf quietened into a long lagoon, was inaccessible for everyone but the ranchers.

"In fact," he said, "they ain't really any towns. Sarita—you passed it but probably didn't notice because it's off the highway a piece—is the county seat, and it's nuthin' but a courthouse and headquarters for the Kenedy Ranch.

"Yessir, this is strictly range country, and there ain't many ranches, 'bout a dozen I'd say. But they cover a lotta ground."

My days were free, and I roamed the length of the coastal plain, visiting the ranches and steeping myself in the lore of the region. The original inhabitants were of course Indians, the inland hunters called Coahuiltecans and the coastal foragers known as Karankawas. The castaway Spaniard Cabeza de Vaca had described the Coahuiltecans as having the keenest eyes and ears in the world, but it was the Karankawas who befriended him and capture our imagination.

I found ways to the island. I used to lie on the beach at Padre and pretend I was a shipwrecked European, looking up to see the Karankawas bearing down on me in one of their great canoes carved from a palm tree. What a fearsome sight they were! Each warrior had half his face painted in red and half in black. Naked but for breechclouts, they were tall and muscular, with pieces of cane pierced through their lips and the nipples of their breasts. My fancy grew out of Noah Smithwick's reality. Even that tough old ranger was moved when in 1900 he saw one of the last Karankawa bands. "They were the most savage looking human beings I ever saw," he wrote. "Many of the bucks were six feet in height, with bows and arrows in proportion. Their ugly faces were rendered hideous by the alligator grease and dirt with which they were besmeared from head to foot as a defense against mosquitoes." For thousands of years they had endured on the coast, surviving the extremes of weather and, in Jesús La Feria's words, "all the things that can get you." And yet within four hundred years after the European intrusion they were gone, decimated by the diseases brought by the white man.

The Spaniards were Medieval men. They sought conquest and treasure in the name of God and civilization, and the Stone Age people of Texas were no match for them. And yet their marriage brought forth the Mexican, the soul of South Texas and the muscle and sinew of ranch life. La Raza is the rawhide that carried the cowboy into our consciousness.

If the Spaniard brought the horse and cow, it was the Mexican who ranched and rodeoed and created the cowboy character. His brand is indelible even today, when most of the great haciendas belong to the Anglo. The gringo may have title, but he is often absent and outnumbered by his Mexican hands. The legendary King Ranch is as famous for its loyal and expert Kinenos as it is for its size and the strength of its fences. Those two old steamboat captains, Richard King and Mifflin Kenedy, were fabulous feudal empire builders, but most of the men who moved their horses and cattle and built their fences bore names like Ramón Alvarado and Luis Robles and Julián Cantú.

And this is what we went searching for on this trip to South Texas: a ranch that still retained the flavor of the old *patrón* and his vaqueros. The King Ranch we passed over because it has been so written about. Almost every outpost was evocative of the Mexican. In Kenedy County alone, most of the spreads had Spanish names: La Paloma, Aquí Paso, Santa Rosa Viejo, La Parra, Carnes-Tolendas, Los Indios, San Pedro, Punta Del Monte, and so on. But it was at the southernmost edge of the county that we found the border Brigadoon.

Twenty-five miles to the east lay the beach, glittering in the waft of the waves that came in from the Gulf of Mexico. Once, 456 years ago, those wind currents and waters had brought to the Boca Chica shore the first white men to Texas. The Spanish came riding top-heavy galleons with gilded windows and dirty heraldic sails. It was September, 1519. They eased up into the mouth of the Rio Grande and anchored. The port in the hull of the head ship opened with a foul yawn, and Captain Alonso Álvarez de Piñeda descended in a small boat. He wore armor, ruffled lace and velvet, and tight leather pants. Soft boots folded about his slender ankles. Something of a dandy. He sprang from the boat, drew his sword, and slashed the water ceremoniously, proclaiming that these waters and this land were the possession of his Most Catholic Majesty, Charles of Spain. And then de Piñeda drove his sword, the sign of the cross, into the sand and knelt before it in prayer. The naked Indians watched in awe. They had never seen such a man. The golden haze of their simple life was about to lift, and we, in a historical sense, were about to begin.

A few miles inland and eighteen generations later, a descendant of that coming together climbed up on a corral gate and shouted instructions to his vaqueros. José Alejandro García spoke in Spanish with the easy authority that comes with aristocracy, but in his dark, hawklike face there was the unmistakable mark of the Indian. He was a small man of seventy, stiffened by bone disease, and yet he gestured and moved with an almost fierce grace, as if to scorn that which afflicted him. He came down off the corral in a cloud of dust. "We are mothering the calves," he said in English. "Come, let's go to the house where it's cool. Maybe Bertha will pour us a beer."

The house sat back five miles off the highway, a relief in the malevolence and monotony of cactus and mesquite. It was small and without distinction, well-kept and comfortable but obviously used as a retreat. The swimming pool, however, was in the grand manner, as was the cabana that sheltered guests.

Bertha García was a handsome matron, as fair as her husband was dark, cool and composed in a light summer frock. She led us to the cabana den. It was a large room full of children in wet bathing suits. They were waiting to kiss their grandfather goodbye. Don José received them like a benign lord. Señora García introduced the two daughters. They were pretty, stylish women who had married Anglos, and the result was pleasing to see in their bright children. Off they went to their homes in Brownsville. "Make yourselves comfortable," Mrs. García said. "And I'll bring you a cold beer."

"Bertha and I try to spend two or three days a week here on the ranch," Don José was saying. "It's very pleasant, especially when all sixteen grandchildren are down for the summer. They like the pool."

He had been born to the good life, you could imagine him saying, and damned if he was going to let a little crippling nuisance spoil his enjoyment of it. He had the *coraje*, the courage. Don José grabbed his cane, swung his way to the Lincoln, and drove out onto the seventy-two-hundred-acre ranch to point out the sights.

The Santa Berta was bounded on the west by the King Ranch, on the south by the Doughtery Ranch, on the east by the ranch of García's sister, María, on the catty-corner by the ranch of his older brother, Miguel, and on the north by the other brother, Martín.

Oh, the Santa Berta was not a large ranch for this part of the country, but it had been in the family for five generations and served as a sentimental retreat as well as a commercially profitable venture. Don José and Bertha lived in Brownsville, where he was a director of a bank and of a savings and loan association. They owned land in four other counties, some with oil wells on it, and had once had half interest in a hundred-thousand-acre rancho in northern Mexico. The agrarians had taken it. Don José served eight years on the Brownsville city commission, and now that that was over, he found himself spending more time at the Santa Berta.

No, he didn't try to run the place himself. At least not alone. His youngest son, José, Jr., helped, and of course there were the vaqueros. They ran about one thousand head of Beefmaster, Charbray, and Limousin cattle, and they bred quarterhorses. No, it didn't take many vaqueros. Right now there were three who lived on the place with their families. Two of the vaqueros, Antonio and Herminio Salinas, were brothers who were born there like their late father, Espedio. Espedio's father, the first Antonio, had found refuge on the ranch after killing a man in San Marcos around the turn of the century. He had remained, working as a *papalotero*, a windmill man, until he died.

"I was just a boy then," Don José said, "but I remember that my mother, Isabel, and my grandfather, Don Pancho, thought highly of the first Antonio. They said he had killed only in self-defense. Anyway, he was a loyal friend to the family. When he approached for instructions, he always removed his sombrero and held it over his breast until he was dismissed. A soldier salutes his superior. It was the *patrón* system, and the son, Espedio, carried it on.

"But Espedio's boys now, they are respectful, but they don't carry it that far. I'd feel kind of silly if they did."

After the brothers there was the old man, Manuel Díaz, a specialist at *trabajo de pie*, footwork, whatever had to be done without being on horseback. "I want you to meet them," Don José said. "There's a good story behind Herminio's birth. He was born on Thanksgiving Day, 1934, and my wife had to help deliver him. The godparents took him to Raymondville to be christened by the padre. But when they got there they couldn't remember what he was to be called. So they named him after Herminio Yturria, one of my step-cousins. When they got back to the ranch they found out that the name was to have been Espedio. They couldn't change what the padre had sprinkled with Holy Water, and he remained Herminio. He has five *niños* now himself. The same thing happened with one of Antonio's boys. He was supposed to have been christened Juan Antonio, but they got confused and called him San Juan. It's on his birth certificate. Saint John!"

Don José drove up in front of a couple of crude but comfortable brick houses with large, ranch-style porches. The porches were packed with playing children. It was too hot out in the sun. The brothers came to the car. Antonio was the taller. Both wore jeans and khaki shirts with a pack of roll-your-own Bugler in the breast pocket. Antonio took the lead in chatting with Don José. I remembered what the old man had said earlier about them, that there was a little friction between them, sibling rivalry. As long as Antonio was giving the orders—as was his due as the foreman—Herminio wasn't much interested in the task at hand. But when Tony was off or sick, Herminio became a very good worker. They returned to the house.

"There's not much to do right now, so they're taking it easy," Don José explained. "They quit at five now. Go to work at eight. Go in at twelve and don't come out until two or three. Have a big siesta, take it easy unless I'm here to bug them. Dependable, but lazier than in the old days, when you worked from sunup to sundown. Now they got television, washing machines. Even butane for cooking and heating. But when they work, nobody can keep up with them. I have to give them credit. A vaquero nowadays has to be more than a rider of horses and a roper of steers, and Antonio and Herminio can do it all. They can weld, lay brick, pour cement. They are carpenters, electricians, plumbers, mechanics, any doggone thing you want them to be. Antonio is as good a *papalotero* as his grandfather was."

"Is that important?"

"A ranch in this country without one is in a hell of a shape. Without water we'd wither. And there isn't much rain. A good windmill man is worth a dozen vaqueros. I'll show you some of our water holes."

The water holes all carried quaint Spanish names. The windmill south of the main ranch house was called Los Ansares, the geese, because a flock always swam there. Another was called Año Nuevo, because the well had been drilled on New Year's Day, and another was Ebonito because a clump of ebony trees grew nearby.

"We call that one over there El Toro Pelón," Don José said, "because a bull without horns died there. And that lake over there is El Estribo, the stirrup, because a vaquero lost a stirrup in it."

How did the ranch come to be called Santa Berta?

"After my wife," he said with a grin. "Bertha is truly a saint."

As he powered the Lincoln through the tangle of mesquite and huisache, Don José talked of his grandfather, Don Pancho Yturria, the patriarch who made the good life possible for his many descendants.

"Don Pancho was born in 1830 in Mexico, the son of an army captain," he said. "He was an educated man—he spoke French, for example—but he was also shrewd in matters of money and soon became a banker and merchant on both sides of the border. He established one of the first banks south of San Antonio. That was in Brownsville in 1867. He also had a bank in Matamoros.

"Don Pancho was an imperialist, and Maximilian, the emperor of Mexico, knighted him and made him the chief of customs for northern Mexico. Padre grande's wealth was beyond measure. He had accounts in banks in Lisbon, London, Hamburg, Liverpool, and New York City. He was a large-scale rancher—plenty to divide among us all—and importer of fine wines and whiskey, and he had lumber interests in Morgan City, Louisiana. You know Reynaldo Garza, the federal judge in Brownsville? Judge Garza's father was Don Pancho's accountant for thirty-five years.

"Don Pancho was one of the incorporators, in 1903, of the St. Louis, Brownsville & Mexico Railway. I remember he used to stop at the ranch in his own private railroad car. He was a short, stocky man with a white beard and a fine sense of humor. Why not? He had made much of life. He married Felicitas Treviño, whose family had land in Hidalgo, Cameron, and Starr counties. They never had any children, so they adopted a son, Daniel, and a daughter, Isabel, my mother.

"Daniel had three sons and a daughter. One of his sons, Fausto, Fausto Yturria, has a ranch across the highway. It was Fausto's son, Junior, who married Sandra Longoria in that big wedding years ago at Brownsville. You probably read about it. There were twelve hundred guests—we went as part of the family—and it was reported in the papers that Shelby Longoria spent $250,000 on his daughter's wedding. Well, he can afford it.

"My mother, Isabel, married Miguel García Decker, a descendant of the founders of San Antonio, and they had five children, too, same as Daniel. Each of us got seventy-two hundred acres in ranchland. When we got down to the household items, my wife thought I would choose Maximilian's bed, a legacy from Don Pancho, because we had slept on it as newlyweds. But I took the painting of Don Pancho, and it hangs over the fireplace in the guest house. My brother Martín got the bed."

Who would get the ranch when he and Bertha were gone?

"Oh, the children," he said. "They already have it, really. The deed is in their names, not ours.

What would happen to Antonio and Herminio and Manuel and their families?

"Why, work here until they die. At least I hope so. Vaqueros are hard to come by. It's getting to be an extinct occupation."

What Don José said was true. The American cowboy evolved into the modern rancher or the rodeo performer, but his Mexican counterpart had no place to go but into town and into another occupation. There was no upward mobility on the *estancia* for a lowly vaquero—security, yes, but no opportunity.

The pastoral life holds no romance for the real rustic. As soon as the vaqueros were able, they fled the ranches for the cities. The few that remain, such as the Salinas brothers, are throwbacks. I could not help but note that Antonio and Herminio wore worn jeans and boots and Texas-style cowboy hats and that they went about their work without the slightest show of flash or machismo. They were sober workmen, *cholos*, not performers. How different they were from the *charro*, the upperclass gentleman who competes in the *charrería* on weekends. Today, in most of the major cities in Texas, you will find *charro* clubs composed of doctors and lawyers and businessmen of Mexican extraction. They don tight-fitting trousers, a short jacket, made-to-order boots to match, an ornate wide-brimmed sombrero, and then go forth to rodeo on purebred horses. Many have developed high skills in the art of *jaripeo* (roping and riding, and so on), and a few of them could probably show Antonio and Herminio a trick or two.

Somewhere between the *peón* and the *patrón* you have the origination of the vaquero, the man on horseback who won the West. It is amazing how quickly the few cows and horses that Cortez brought over multiplied, and how within twenty years after the Conquest the first great cattle ranches were taking over the land of New Spain. By the end of the sixteenth century, European Samuel de Champlain wrote that he was astounded by the "great, level plains, stretching endlessly and everywhere covered with an infinite number of cattle." As early at 1554 the Indian inhabitants of Cholula were complaining to the Crown that "the many cattle *estancias* are ruining us and putting poor *macehuales* [native farmers] to flight." The viceroy's most pressing problem was to keep *estancias* away from villages and to keep cattle out of the Indians' maize.

Cattle raising became the colony's economic lifeblood. Meat consumption increased; even the Indians began to eat it. But most of the cattle were slaughtered for their hides, which was New Spain's greatest export. The leather from the new world outfitted the great Spanish armies. The great ranches extended from the torrid zone to the remote northern reaches. The first cowboy was called an *estanciero*, a slightly derogatory connotation which represented white men at the bottom of the social scale, or sometimes mestizos, Negroes, or mulattoes. These *hombres a caballo* worked for fixed wages or for a *partido* of the profits. Independent, restless, they moved from one lonely outpost to another and came to be called vaqueros.

To kill the cattle they used a crescent-shaped blade mounted on a long pole. A *desjarretadera*. They would gallop up to a steer and cut its hamstrings without dismounting. In 1607 a New Galicia government inspector wrote of the vaqueros: "They are called saddletree lads because their sole possessions are a wretched old saddle, a lightly stepping mare, usually stolen, and their lance. They, however, insist on being called vaqueros. They strike terror to the heart of the population. They ride about in bands and no one dares withstand them."

Not every vaquero was a vagabond. As the country grew more civilized, the owners themselves began to take up residence on the *estancias*. They hired steadier, less independent vaqueros, most of whom now were Indians. This was the beginning of the haciendas, where farming was combined with ranching around a great plantation house inhabited by the *patrón*. On these great estates the peons and their families lived like vassals in a feudal system. The vaqueros were a little freer. Here they refined the skills with horses and bulls that the early Texans would come to emulate. The cowboy not only copied the vaquero in his culture—the rodeo, saddle, stirrups, spurs and lariat, language; he also took on many of his character traits. They both were low-class, but independent as hell.

Don José was a *patrón* without apology. It had come to him out of the continuity of blood and breeding to make what he could with inheritance. It had not been easy. Command never is. That it had been profitable was both providential and proof of their prudence. The family motto was not "Cum Deo et Honore" for nothing.

"As for the vaqueros," he said, "they feel and we feel they are part of the family. It is the old way. They feel this is their place. They live here all the time, and they know the place better than I do. Their dead, from the first Antonio on, are buried out there in the mesquite.

"But everything is changing. Go down in the valley. Most political jobs are held by the Latin. I don't consider myself exactly a Latin. By Mexican custom I happen to have a Latin last name—my mother's—but remember my father was German, a Decker. I'm a lot of things, but what I am finally is simply an American. La Raza, bah! If they want to be Mexican, let them go to Mexico. Forget the race and be Americans. I don't know, maybe we're getting lazy, letting the minorities take over. Oh, it'll all even out some day. Maybe there might be a revolution."

I asked him if he worried about the loyalty of his vaqueros.

"You never know," he said philosophically. "A smooth-talking labor organizer might come along and talk Antonio into something. Maybe because he hasn't realized what a good deal he's got here. When I first took over, all they got was $18 a month and rations. They're making $250 a month now, and we still butcher the animals for them. Every morning before the school bus comes Herminio and his wife and children milk my cows. They drink a little of the milk and make cheese out of the rest. Then they take the cheese into town and sell it. It shows industry on their part, so I never interfere. They keep what they make. Everything else is free—their houses, water, lights, the trucks they drive, and even the gas for their own personal cars. They each own two cars apiece.

"I don't know now what they get in stamps from the government, but I think it comes close to another two hundred dollars a month. Hell, they got a better hat than I do. They ride my horses, and you know what? I can't sell them without their permission!"

Raymondville, 1975

The Folk Singer Who Sang Opera

He stood on the roadside in the rain, a guitar in one hand and a suitcase in the other.

They laughed at the coincidence and stopped to pick him up. He grinned broadly and climbed in. He was tall and dressed like a cowboy actor down on his luck. His belly hung over his belt, and when he took off his broad-brimmed hat, a shower of thin, gray hair fell over his big ears.

"Guy, this is crazy," one of them said with a grin. "Here we are on our way to Austin to interview a country music singer, and we run into you. Don't tell me you sing like Jimmy Rodgers, too."

"As a matter of fact I can," he said with an arch of his eyebrows. "Shall I?"

"Sure."

He wiped the water from his guitar, strummed the strings, and sang in a voice like Jimmy's:

> All around a water tank
> Awaitin' for a train
> A thousand miles away from home
> A'sleepin' in the rain. . . .

They laughed like little boys with a new toy.

"Rupert Spencer's the name," he said. "But just call me Jack."

"Where'ya headed, Jack?"

"San Antonio. Hoping to find work there."

"Sing for a living?"

"Yes sir, and you're kind to call it singing. I thank you."

"Don't apologize. You sound real good."

"I appreciate that. Really do. Yes sir."

"Gonna catch up with a band?"

"No sir. I'm I guess what you'd call a loner. I move from town to town, picking up a few bucks here and there, mostly in beer joints and bars."

"Where'd you play last night?"

"Somewhere in North Houston. Mac's Place, I think."

"Was it profitable?"

"You shouldn't ask him a personal question like that."

"Oh, that's quite all right. I don't mind saying. I picked up four dollars and a night's room rent before they had a fight in the place."

"You didn't get involved?"

"Oh no. I'm too old for that."

"How old are you, Jack?"

"Sixty-two."

"Sixty-two? That's my age. Well son-of-a-gun! What month?"

"May. May 18th."

"I'm May 13!"

"Awww . . . really? Wonderful. You're Taurus too. Old bull Taurus."

"Taurus smarus. I don't believe in that junk. You do?"

"Oh, astronomy is a true science."

"It's astrology, not astronomy. And it's pure nonsense."

"Well, you could be right . . . I. . . ."

"How long you been on the road, guy?"

"Forty years."

"Like it?"

"Yessir, I do. I have to say I do."

"Don't you get kind of lonesome sometimes?"

"Well, I love people. Love to meet people and go places I never been. I never meet a stranger."

"No family?"

"Oh, I got a family, fine family. My wife Minnie is chief cashier in a bank in New Orleans, and my son, he's twenty-one, is studying to be an engineer."

"How often do you see them?"

"I spend about three months out of the year with them. The rest of the time I'm on the road."

"What do they think about you wanderin' around the country like this?"

"Oh Minnie understands me. So does my boy, Bruce. They're wonderfully understanding."

"Guy, you're all right. You're all right."

"Well thank you, sir. Thank you. You fellows are all right, too. What line of work are you in?"

"Bill here's a newspaperman, and I'm a writer. He's going to do the story on the folk singer in Austin."

"Jack, do another song for us."

"Would you like to hear some opera?"

"Opera? You sing opera?"

"I'll let you gentlemen be the judge."

He reared back and bellowed a few bars from Verdi. He was Rhadames expressing his love for Aïda. He had once had a good tenor voice. That was obvious. It was heavier now, a mite rusty and thin on the high notes.

But they were dumbfounded, and he was proud. He was a different man now. He launched into *Rigoletto*, "T'amo ripetilo!" He gestured like Caruso, making little O signs with his fingers as he strained to reached the high notes.

"You hear that?" he asked. "I hit a B natural. That's as high as most tenors go today. People think it's a high C, but it's really a B natural. It's hard to tell the difference."

He sang arias and talked opera as the miles ticked away on the speedometer. He said he was one-quarter Pawnee Indian, originally from Oklahoma, but that he had spent most of his early life in New York, studying singing under a J. H. Duval, whom he described as one of the world's great voice teachers.

He dug into his suitcase and pulled out piles of opera scores. They were worn from use and filled with his own phonetic notations. He showed equally worn pictures of his wife and son and asked if he could accompany his newfound friends to Austin.

"I never meet gentlemen like you in the places I sing," he

said. "They laugh at me when I sing opera. So I stick to the hill-billy and pop tunes. But opera is my love. I have little money, but I will do anything you want me to do and will not be a burden."

"Knock it off, guy. Sure, you're welcome. Glad to have you along."

The weekend in Austin was like one of those Steinbeck would think up for his peons in the Salinas Valley.

One of them made a remark about the gravy stains on Jack's cowboy shirt, so he took his paltry wardrobe to a washateria and bellowed an aria from *Salomé* while his socks and underwear washed and spun dry.

His voice was getting better. "You know," he said, "I believe if I could vocalize for about six weeks and get my voice in shape, I could sing opera for some small company. If I could just get a stake. . . ."

He amused the celebrants at a victory brawl for Senator Ralph Yarborough, then accompanied the crowd to Threadgill's, a gas station turned tavern where Austin's famous Jimmy Rodgers fan, Ken Threadgill, holds forth.

Jack was properly subdued at Threadgill's and had to be told only once to stop singing because somebody wanted to hear Ken.

"What'ya think of Threadgill?" he was asked.

"Oh, he's got that Rodgers style down," he admitted. "Yodel's real fine. But, well, I just don't care for imitators."

"I don't imitate Jimmy," Threadgill said later. "Our voices break the same way on a yodel, but Jimmy's voice was shriller than mine. Jimmy had what I'd call a Cajun brogue, while I've got kind of a Texas drawl. Jimmy sang 'Never No Mo' Blues' in B-flat. I do it in G. We keep a straight rhythm, and Jimmy broke his."

The next morning, Jack and his two *compadres* marched boldly into Seton Hospital, four hours ahead of visiting hours, to cheer author Fred Gipson, who lay like a wounded bull in a third-floor bed.

Jack sang *Rigoletto* at the top of his register, and Gipson roared approval. They harmonized on some cowboy songs while the hospital people stood outside the door wringing their hands but holding their peace.

On the road back to Houston, too many slugs of red whiskey spun Jack's head around and set his ulcers on fire. "I wish I was home with Minnie and Bruce," he said.

After some hot coffee, he got to feeling like his old self again. He launched into a medicine show pitch.

"Now friends," he barked, "I wish you would stand in a little closer to the platform. Don't block the sidewalk. I want to introduce you to Dr. Zackankack's extract of the root of a root of a toot bush.

"We found it forty miles from land or water in the wilds of Africa and guarantee it will make you root and toot. It's good for man or beast externally or internally and can't hurt the most delicate system. It won't rip, rust, ravel, or run down at the heels or smell bad in warm weather. It takes off warts, whelps, and all blemishes from the skin...."

And on it went.

When Jack got out of the car, he shook hands around, and all swore to get together again, although each knew it would never happen.

As he walked away and up the steps of the shabby hotel, the wind caught his hair and bared a big bald spot on the back of his head. Somehow he looked vulnerable. They hoped he would make it home to Minnie, if that was where he wanted to go.

Austin, 1964

Old Juan

The gringos had not paid much attention to Old Juan over the years, but now as they grew old and indolent and watched him pass on the roadside, pulling his little cart in search of bottles to sell, they began to realize that he had been a man when they were children.

"Why, I am sixty-five," D. C. Eskew said, "and I can remember Old John when I was about ten. He worked in the fields for Dad and he looked old to me then. 'Course anyone over twenty looks old to a kid."

"Well, I'm climbing the ladder pretty high," Eskew's sister, Gertrude Brodie, who will be eighty-one in April, said, "and I was a kid when Old John was stealing chickens from us. Now I shouldn't say that. Never had any proof. But ever' time we'd return from town, a fryer'd be missing, and we always figured it was Old John."

Mae Herndon said they'd always called him Tin John. "Goodness knows how old he is, but I guess he's lived out there in that mesquite thicket for fifty, sixty years. Had him a hole in the ground with a piece of tin over it. There must have been some tie between him and Grandpa, because Grandpa never chased John off. He'd do chores for us, work in the field sometimes, but he never said much and always kept to himself."

Grandpa was Old Man Joe Davis, a respected rancher in those days, and the mesquite thicket where Old Juan lived was on the Davis spread, just southwest of Austin, in the pasture cornered by Davis and Brodie lanes. Old Man Davis had been dead since 1924, and a Dr. W. W. Harris owned the place now.

He was not as close to the old Mexican as Davis had been, but he let Old Juan remain in the thicket.

Country people are not nosy; it is when they move into town that they start prying into other people's business. The gringos who knew Old Juan lived at the edge of Austin, but the town had come to them, not they to it, and they had kept their country ways. Old Juan interested them only when he came into view, and then it was his age, rather than the man himself, that intrigued them. So they speculated. What they knew of Old Juan himself could be said in a minute. He was old as Genesis, stooped as *Pithecanthropus erectus,* and the damndest pedestrian in Travis County. Almost every morning he would emerge from the thicket and start walking, his tiny wheeled cart trailing behind. He collected his bottles and cashed them in at grocery stores along whatever route he was taking. Dusk would find him five or ten miles from his burrow in the thicket, but he always managed to hoof it back.

This had been Old Juan's routine for years, since the Model T truck Old Man Davis had given him had conked out. What else did they know? Well, one winter he had almost frozen in his hole—would have if someone hadn't found him. Another time there had been a fire in the thicket, and Old Juan had had to haul in newer old lumber for another roof. He never spoke English, but they figured he knew more than he let on.

That was it—all they knew of a man and a neighbor they had seen almost daily for a lifetime. They did not even know his last name.

One among them, a newcomer, found this situation distressing. It seemed to him that common decency, if not curiosity, would compel them to take more interest in the old recluse. He thought he had noticed that Old Juan walked with a limp and that his tattered clothes were too thin for the October mornings. Was the old Mexican well? Had he clothes enough and shelter for the coming winter? People should be more concerned!

The gringo took it upon himself to visit Old Juan. Even if the old man had no material wants, surely he would welcome company. He might turn out to be a very interesting man, you could never tell. A man doesn't shift for himself out in the wild and not develop some character. Perhaps Old Juan was a Mexican Thoreau, a poet in the rough. To make sure he and the old man would understand each other, the gringo asked a Mexican friend, Tomás Govea, to accompany him. Tomás was an humble man with a rare insight into people, and how he loved to talk!

Tomás had a bachelor friend named Gomez, and when Tomás told him what he was about to do, Gomez blinked. A tear rolled down his cheek. Gomez had a soft heart. He was already sorry for Old Juan without seeing him. Imagine! To live like a dog in the woods! Ignored, unloved! Gomez sighed. That could very well happen to him in his old age, for he had no one either. "It is not the same thing," Tomás assured him. "You will never come to that." Gomez wanted to meet Old Juan, too, but he could not take off from work. Tomás thought it was just as well. Gomez took things too personally.

The next day the gringo and Tomás left their car on Brodie Lane, climbed through a barbed-wire fence, and approached the mesquite thicket.

"Señor Juan, Señor Juan," they called.

A dog barked.

They stopped at the edge and peered in. In the center of the thicket was a clearing. They could make out a small *jacal* built low and into the ground like a pillbox. Its waist-high roof was made of branches and bits of tin and cloth and held a smokestack. It was difficult to see the growling dog for all the rubbish that was strewn about—mounds of broken and rusted objects that would have been worthless to anyone but a scavenger. A car was parked halfway into the clearing. No, it was a frail Model T Ford pickup, and it wasn't parked; it had taken root in rust and was growing back into the earth, returning to ore again. A tin Dorian Gray. A morning dew lay upon the thicket, and horny-backed spiders, quivering tinctures of topaz, hung from the mesquite ceiling on silvery snares almost too fine to be seen. The door of the *jacal* wobbled open. Old Juan stuck out his head. He hushed the dog and looked in the direction of the callers. "*Quién?*" he croaked. Who?

"Good morning, sir," Tomás called out in Spanish. "With your permission, we would like to speak with you."

"*Un momento,*" the old man said, and presently he was before them, a tiny wraith of a man, no higher than a boy, brown of face and bent of body. He blinked in the light and rubbed his eyes. Everything about him bespoke age and hard times. Everything about him drooped: his heavy white hair, his itching old eyes and the bags beneath them, his nose, his moustache, his mouth, his shoulders, the second-hand clothes he wore. It was awkward. Old Juan did not greet his visitors. He didn't say a word. He stood before them scratching at his eyes with a fist as stiff and stained as a rodent's paw. At last he said, "*Pues?*" Well then?

Tomás held out a brown paper sack. "We have brought a gift of groceries, sir. Nothing much. Some potatoes. Bread. Tamales. Tobacco. We got Bugler, roll your own, because we didn't know...."

"*Está bueno,*" Old Juan said. "It is the kind I use."

And to show that he was not *mal criado*, that he was not ill-bred, Old Juan invited them into the clearing. He seemed to sense right away that the men meant him no harm, that they had just come to talk and to look him over. Well, he would abide them. But the gringo he ignored. He was not rude, he was just indifferent, which is the worst affront of all. He responded to Tomás, however. They were countrymen, and the old man admitted he got lonesome once in a while for his own people. All the Mexicans had moved to town, and he had not been there in years. He hated the pueblo, any pueblo. He had always been a *campesino*. Ay! A man after Tomás's own heart. Tomás lived in town, but he had always worked in the country for the ranchers. They compared former employers. The talk went well between them, and the gringo was content to listen.

The old man's name was Juan Torres, and he remembered coming down out of the Sierra Madre, the eastern range in the state of Tamaulipas, when he was about nine to cross over the border into Texas. It was a mistake, he said. After his family settled in the hills near San Marcos, he fell ill. A terrible sickness seized his stomach and then spread all over his body from the neck down. He was only a boy, but he never regained his health. That, he said, was why he never married. His sisters found mates and moved away, and when his parents died, Juan moved into the thicket on the Davis place.

"When was that?" Tomás asked.

"It has been fifty years."

"The gringos around here say you may have a hundred years or more," Tomás said.

"Ah!" the old man said. "No. *Setenta y cinco.*" Seventy-five.

"In what year were you born?"

He replied, without hesitation, that it was 1893.

"That would give you seventy-five years all right," Tomás said, squatting on the ground. The old man had already eased himself down. He drew out a rusty pocketknife and began cutting at the stems of weeds. "The gringos must be confused," Tomás decided. Old Juan shrugged.

Tomás grew philosophical.

"You have lived a long time," he said, "and you have had to be alone with yourself and your thoughts. What advice would you give a young man?"

"*Nada,*" Old Juan said. Nothing.

Tomás protested. The more years one had, the more wisdom he had.

Old Juan scoffed and shook his head. Such folly! He dug at his swollen eyes. "It is not true," he said. "The years do the same thing to an old man's head that whiskey does to a drunk. They make him confused and worthless."

Tomás, who knew well the sin in gin, liked that. "But you, sir," he said. "You don't imbibe?"

"I like beer," Old Juan said.

"But you have learned nothing in life?" Tomás pressed.

Well, he had decided it was best to work in order to eat, because if you stole to eat you would end up in jail.

Tomás laughed.

"How would you describe your life out here?" Tomás went on, "good or bad in the eyes of God?"

"Neither good nor bad," Old Juan said.

"You do believe in God?"

"Sí, everybody believes in God."

"And the devil?"

Old Juan smiled. "The devils are many and God is one, and there is more evidence of devils. There are devils of men and devils of the spirit."

"Ay . . . very true," Tomás said. "I can name some right now."

"I heard the *brujas* the other night," Old Juan said.

"Witches?"

"Sí, they made strange noises."

"Like how?"

"Like a flapping of wings. They moved across the pasture. They spoke in Spanish this time, but last year they spoke in English."

"What did they say?"

"I could not get it."

"Were you afraid?"

"No."

"I would be," Tomás said. He was in earnest. "I'm a chicken. I don't want to die."

"I don't want to die," Old Juan said. "But I am not afraid."

"Life gives you pleasure then?"

"No. My life has been very bad. I have not enjoyed it."

"Is it because you are alone?"

"No. I like being alone."

"Then it is your poverty?"

"No. Countrymen are always poor. I have known nothing else. It is the sickness. I have not been strong since I had nine years."

"But you walk miles!"

"I do it out of necessity, not out of strength. I have to find bottles and sell them or starve."

"You receive no government aid?"

"No. I know nothing of that. I did not bother to get my citizen papers."

"You deserve. . . ."

"I deserve nothing but what I can get by my own hand. I accept your groceries, but it is better for me that I work for them. It is the only thing that keeps me going, the need to work."

"You have never been happy?"

"When I was a Juanito in the mountains. That was a sweet time. But Texas ruined me. I became a viejo before my time. I think it was the food. It did something to my stomach. I have never gotten over it."

Tomás threw in one more question. "If you could have anything you wanted now, what would it be?"

"Steady work and a water well," Old Juan said.

"Where do you get your water?" Tomás asked.

"From a cow trough in the pasture," Old Juan replied. He turned and looked toward his *jacal.* "It is time for you to go now," he said. "I have things to attend to. I have to go to the store."

"Allow us to take you," Tomás offered. "We will even bring you back."

Old Juan shook his head in irritation, but then he reconsidered. He said he needed a new hat, but hadn't gotten one because he did not want to walk into Austin. He repeated his distaste for the city. He would ride with them, however, if they would drop him off at some second-hand store. He did not want them to return him home. He preferred to walk. He would take the cart and collect bottles on the way home.

They waited while he "locked up." Some gringo boys had been stealing things from his *jacal.* They would watch him leave and then raid it. The dog was of no use. It belonged to someone else and only came to visit him.

Old Juan's manner of locking up left Tomás scratching his head. Old Juan had no lock, so he secured the door with rusty wire. He donned a hat that must have come with the 1917 Ford truck. The crown had rotted out, and he had sewn it in again. He clutched a small coin purse in one paw and pulled his cart to the car with the other.

On the way in, the gringo, who had been ignored but who still felt sorry for the old Mexican, decided he would insist on paying for the hat and anything else Old Juan wanted. It did not work out as he had planned.

They looked at hats at the Goodwill store, at the Saint Vincent de Paul shop, and at the Salvation Army, but none suited Old Juan, although many were good fits and in better shape than the fermenting felt he wore.

Old Juan was very jumpy, almost testy. The traffic in the streets bothered him, and he seemed to get claustrophobia if a store was the slightest bit crowded. They met Gomez, Tomás's soft-hearted friend, on the street, and although Gomez acted very pleased to meet him, Old Juan just looked sour.

But as it was Old Juan's first trip into town in years, he apparently did not want to go back home empty-handed. Shoes! He wanted to buy some shoes. But once inside, the old man would give the rows of toed-up rejects a half-hearted inspection and limp toward the exit. The shoes he wore were lopsided with wear and tear, but apparently he preferred them to the others. On the sidewalk he suddenly turned to Tomás and thanked him and said he had to be on his way.

"Allow us at least to take you out on the highway," Tomás insisted. Old Juan sighed and got into the car. They told him not to worry about not finding a hat and shoes, that they would buy him some and bring them out to the thicket. What was his size?

Old Juan declined. A man should not buy shoes without trying them on. The same with a hat. He urged them to forget the idea and let him out at the next corner.

Tomás helped him set his cart on the sidewalk.

"Are you sure you can find your way back?"

Sí, he was sure.

"I realize we may have made too many demands on your time today," Tomás said, "and I apologize. But the next time we come we will bring some beer, ah, and not stay so long."

"I really don't like beer or company all that much," the old man said. "I would consider it a favor if you did not come back to see me."

And with that he waved his hand in a good-bye and started off down the sidewalk, his wagon clattering behind.

Tomás looked at the gringo and grinned.

Austin, 1969

The Aurora Spaceman

Wise County, Texas, lies just north of where the West begins, upon a pretty little promontory which divides the Grand Prairie and the Western Cross Timbers. There the town of Aurora once was.

I say *was* because it's gone now, has been for more than seventy years. Oh, there are still a few people around, but the only businessman left is Brawley Oates, and Mr. Oates is not exactly setting the world on fire. If things continue as they have, Brawley will end his days in that little Arco service station, the only gas stop between Boyd and Rhome. Those are towns to the east and west, towns that made it when Aurora couldn't, if you call a few hundred people coming together and hanging on for dear life making it.

But back to Brawley Oates.

The one in the gas station, not the two in the cemetery. You see, the family goes back some. The first Brawley Oates— he was a lean old patriarch with a long white beard—was in this county, and a power to be reckoned with, as early as 120 years ago. The point is that the Oateses are a patient people who don't run away when the going gets tough. And this place has had it, a number of times, through the years.

But now things are looking up.

People are starting to pay attention to Aurora again, to buy gasoline from Brawley.

And it's all because of the man from Mars who is buried in the local cemetery.

Well, I don't believe it, but a lot of people do, and that's what all the fuss is about—whether to dig him up or not. The good ladies and gentlemen of the Aurora Cemetery Association say let him lie in peace, whoever or whatever he is. And they are so adamant about it they've gone to a lawyer over in Decatur, which is the county seat, and had papers drawn up to try to prevent disturbance of any body in the cemetery.

On the other side are some characters who call themselves UFO experts and who identify themselves as being with various unidentified flying object networks. They haven't actually tried it yet, but it is obvious they are itching to go at Aurora Cemetery with picks and shovels. They've been hovering about the graves for weeks with metal detectors and other witching rods, and they are convinced that this grave—or if not this one then some other in the cemetery—holds the secret of the so-called man from outer space.

The sole authority for all this rests on a seven-paragraph story which appeared on page five of the *Dallas Morning News*, and on page four of the *Fort Worth Record*, on Monday, April 19, 1897. Seventy-six years ago! Well let's go back and read it, in full. The dateline was Aurora, Wise County, Texas, April 17, 1897, and the story went as follows:

About six o'clock this morning the early risers of Aurora were astonished at the sudden appearance of the airship which has been sailing through the country.

It was traveling due north, and much nearer the earth than ever before. Evidently some of the machinery was out of order, for it was making a speed of only ten or twelve miles an hour and gradually getting toward the earth. It sailed directly over the public square, and when it reached the north part of town collided with the tower of Judge Proctor's windmill and went to pieces with a terrible explosion, scattering debris over several acres of ground, wrecking the windmill and water tank and destroying the judge's flower garden.

The pilot of the ship is supposed to have been the only one on board, and while his remains are badly disfigured, enough of the original has been picked up to show that he was not an inhabitant of this world.

Mr. T. J. Weems, the United States Signal Service officer at this place and an authority on astronomy, gives it as his opinion that he was a native of the planet Mars.

Papers found on his person—evidently the record of his travels—

are written in some unknown hieroglyphics, and cannot be deciphered.

The ship was too badly wrecked to form any conclusion as to its construction or motive power. It was built of an unknown metal, resembling somewhat a mixture of aluminum and silver, and it must have weighed several tons.

The town is full of people to-day who are viewing the wreck and gathering specimens of the strange metal from the debris. The pilot's funeral will take place at noon tomorrow.

That was the story, and the man who filed it signed his name at the bottom, S. E. Haydon. Haydon, it turns out, was an Aurora cotton buyer who on occasion served as a country correspondent for the city newspapers.

From time to time in the years since, when local news was slow and the national scene was depressing, feature writers have tended to dig up Mr. Haydon's old item and give it another run for the money, usually at UFO time, when, for whatever reasons—perhaps spring and the running sap and the pulling moon —there is a rash of flying saucer reports and people begin to imagine that we are being visited by creatures from outer space. Jerry Flemmons of the *Fort Worth Star-Telegram* has probably gotten more mileage out of the Aurora spaceman than anyone, having sold the story to a dozen publications since 1966, and yet Flemmons has never taken the tale seriously.

In fact no reporter had until Bill Case of the *Dallas Times Herald* came driving into Aurora one day last March wearing an Apollo flight jacket and a semiscientific mien in his manner.

Case is an old Hearst-UPI man who came to the *Times Herald* several years ago to wind up a long reporting career in aviation, aerospace, and medicine. On the surface, he gives an impression of deliberation and objectivity. (Give me the facts, Ma'am, only the observed and proven data.) But I sense in Bill the heart of the romantic, a true believer, whose approach to— well, to the Aurora spaceman—is more intuitive than critical. In other words, he came to Aurora a partisan, and not, in my view, a detached observer. I have done the same thing on other stories about subjects dear to my heart. We all do it from time to time.

But the people's impression of Bill Case, when he hit Aurora, was the opposite of mine. He looked very official. In fact, from a distance one resident took him to be either the dog catcher or the highway patrol. Olive khaki shirt, khaki trousers, metal-rimmed sun glasses. The off-white car with a hard hat in the rear window. Upon closer inspection, Mr. Case was obviously with the National Aeronautics and Space Administration. He wore their insignias on his jacket. That was the rumor that went around, and some Aurorans who had scoffed at the legend of the spaceman began to have second thoughts.

In orbit with Case were several other investigators: Hayden Hewes and Tommy Blann with the International Unidentified Flying Objects Bureau out of Oklahoma City; Earl F. Watts of Duncanville, state director of astronomy for MUFON, the Midwest Unidentified Flying Object Network; and Fred N. Kelley, whom Case identified as a treasure hunter and lost metal locator from Corpus Christi. Their titles were impressive, but when one saw their cars parked around Brawley Oates's service station, cars and campers with more surreal equipment than a deputy sheriffs' convention painted by Dali, one could only echo Mrs. Edith Brown's reaction. "They're getting me to where I'm about to believe them," she said. "I didn't think they would ever go to the moon, but they did!"

The attention was focused around Brawley Oates because Brawley lives on the place where the airship was reported to have crashed back in '97. The house is up on the hill just behind the service station, and back of it is the well where our science writer—or science fiction writer, if you will, our late, great Mr. Haydon—wrote that the airship landed. A galactic Quixote, doing battle with windmills.

Of course the windmill is gone, and over the well is a pump house which Brawley Oates has converted into a chicken coop. You know, Brawley has some good chickens in there, some Domineckers and White Leghorns and Rhode Island Reds, but look at them! They haven't any better sense than we have, scratching away for a worm they won't find.

Well this is where the so-called scientific scratching has been going on, the search for some bit of metal, some piece of proof that old S. E. Haydon was not a liar.

That, essentially, is what has been going on here in Aurora, Texas, since March. Bill Case or one of the grandsons of Brawley Oates leading the curious through a bunch of chicken . . . feathers.

Oh, some metal has been found, metal other than shotgun shell caps, old stove lids, and horse bridle rings. The other day, Benny Rasberry, Brawley Oates's twelve-year-old grandson, found a silver half-dollar, minted in New Orleans, dated 1856. And Case and some of the other UFO experts have dug up fragments which seem to excite them a great deal.

Back in April, the treasure hunter, Fred Kelley, unearthed twelve pieces of a lightweight metal which he said was unlike any metal he had ever seen.

And right after that, Case and the UFO men spotted what they feel is the grave of the spaceman.

What led them to it, Case said, were directions from an old-timer Case refuses to unmask with an identification. The other clue that led them to the grave in question was the unusual marking on the headstone: no name or anything, not S. E. Haydon's "unknown hieroglyphics," but clearly, at least clearly to Bill Case, the crude imprint of a spaceship carved into the stone. Case even sees port windows in the drawing. What I see is a line of cracks which could be a spaceship if you wanted it to be, but it's clearly an if-you-want-it-to-be thing, and Case's port windows seem to be circles of fossil in the rock. Whatever, the plot thickened when Earl Watts's metal detector was held over the grave and registered the same readings as those shown by the metal found at the well site.

That was enough for Hayden Hewes of the IUFOB of Oklahoma to tell Case, and the world, "We are more convinced than ever that a UFO crashed here and that the pilot was killed and buried in this cemetery. Our attorneys are already checking to learn how we might have the body exhumed."

Hewes, a dramatic fellow who wore white boots (were Flash Gordon's boots white?), then took his metal samples and dematerialized back to Oklahoma.

The trustees of the cemetery, taking Mr. Hewes at his word, called out Wise County Sheriff Eldon Moyers to stand guard at the cemetery. Then they retained Decatur attorney Bill Nobles to fight any attempt to exhume the body.

But is there a body, earthly or unearthly, beneath that makeshift stone? Cemetery records only show that a man named C. A. Carr owned the plot. Carr's descendants cannot be found, so we don't know if Carr is buried there or somewhere else. Lynn McCrary, a local welder, is president of the cemetery association, and he says a lot of people are buried there in unmarked or unidentified graves. During the 1890's people around here were dying from spotted fever and yellow fever, and many were buried quickly with no headstones.

How that particular and peculiar stone came to be over that grave, if indeed it is a grave, is a mystery. Apparently it's been there a long time, if City Marshal H. R. Idell's memory serves.

Idell says the stone has been there since he was a kid. He also mentions that he cleaned out the well on Judge Proctor's place, where the airship is supposed to have crashed, back in 1945, when Brawley Oates bought the place and moved onto it, and that he found pieces of metal in the well that look like the stuff Case and the UFO people have found.

The reason Brawley Oates wanted the well cleaned was because he and his family wanted to drink from it. It had not been used in years. Well, they drank from it for twelve years. Then they quit. There was something about it that made them uneasy. An accumulation of misfortunes that may or may not have had anything to do with the well and its water.

First their youngest daughter, Sarah Lenora, died at the age of nine months of a sickness the doctor could not pinpoint, although a polio epidemic was going on at the time. Then Brawley and his wife Bonnie developed arthritis, which in Brawley's case took on monstrous proportions when it was complicated by goiter.

The other day, during all this flap about the spaceman and the well and the cemetery, some sightseer who gassed up at Brawley's pumps wondered aloud if maybe it wasn't radiation that had caused Brawley's medical problems. This is an example of how the story of the Aurora spaceman has gathered momentum. Momentum and mutation.

Out of a meaningless mosaic of fragments, Bill Case has fashioned a fantastic feature story which, coming as it has during the dog days of summer and Watergate, has been welcomed by readers around the world as well as by those here in Dallas and Fort Worth. Case is keeping a scrapbook of all the places that are picking up on his story. The *Times Herald* has recognized this and has permitted him voyage. Since March, Case and the Aurora spaceman have been in the paper almost every other day, often on the front page. Each new development is reported with the earnestness of straight news, as if it is indeed a fact that men of science are taking it seriously.

Case is a smooth old pro when it comes to adjectives. "Highly sensitive" is one phrase that runs through his accounts of Mr. Watts's divining. This kind of emphasis tends to imbue a $150 instrument with more savvy than it has. The same with Case's reporting of the laboratory tests on the metal dug up. It has not undergone mere analyses, but rather "intensive" analyses. When he brings the treasure hunter, Fred Kelley, into the picture, he is careful to point out that Mr. Kelley is a "scientific" treasure hunter. The airship on the tombstone was "laboriously carved" into the rock.

The other day, on page one of his paper, Bill Case reported that scientists had analyzed metal fragments from the well and that they had concluded that it was an alloy which could not have been produced on earth until the twentieth century.

This indeed is earth-shaking news as long as you forget that 1897 was but three years away from the present century. Or as long as you don't want to know the identity of the scientists who checked the metal. Case identifies them only as people from one of the nation's leading aircraft manufacturers. He has to protect their names, he says, because, as he puts it, "You know what the government's attitude is toward UFOs."

Case is one of those people who believe that the U.S. government is supressing evidence that flying saucers are indeed real and that they could be reconnaissance missions for an invasion from outer space.

Here we must add, not incidentally, that Bill Case is, by his own admission, an investigator and consultant to MUFON, the Mid-West Unidentified Flying Object Network.

To lend even more credence to this posture of scientific inquiry, Case and the *Times Herald* announced that Dr. J. Allen Hynek, chairman of Northwestern University's astronomy department, will take leave of Evanston, Illinois, and descend upon Aurora, Texas, "to evaluate the evidence."

Dr. Hynek, who is MUFON's chief consultant, was quoted as saying: "We have been following the scientific search of this site and the cemetery with great interest. Now looking at this most recent evidence it highly suggests the actual crash of an aerial object did occur.

"In view of both the identification of the metal and the testimony of some of the most highly respected members of pioneer families in the area who have given details of the reported crash, the likelihood that this is a hoax seems more and more improbable."

Well I haven't met Dr. Hynek, but I can't help but notice that he talks like Bill Case writes.

Thus far, in four months of trying, not even Mr. Case has been able to come up with an eyewitness to the crash. The closest he has come are three or four old-timers who say they remember talk of such a crash. Charlie Stephens, an eighty-year-old Aurora farmer, is typical of them.

It is uncanny to me, or maybe it's canny, that no one has explored, at least not in print, the character of the three men who were in on the story from the beginning seventy-six years ago.

That would be S. E. Haydon, the Aurora cotton buyer who wrote the original story in the Dallas and Fort Worth papers; Judge J. S. Proctor, into whose windmill the airship was supposed to have crashed; and T. J. Weems, whom Haydon identified in the story as a "United States Signal Service officer and an authority on astronomy." Weems, you remember, was the one who decided that the spaceman was a Martian.

Let's begin with Jeff Weems. There is no record or recollection that he was ever a Signal Service officer, much less an authority on astronomy. Mr. Haydon, it appears, was having some fun with the local blacksmith, for that was what T. J. Weems was—the local farrier. Weems eventually moved to Rhome, where he ran a grocery store until his death in 1925 at the age of eighty-two.

But before we go on to the other two partners in this vintage bit of interstellar horseplay, let's go back and look at the context in which Haydon's story was played in the *Dallas News*.

The story, as we said earlier, ran on page five, buried down toward the middle of a page that contained no fewer than sixteen reports from as many area towns about an airship being sighted. Remember, this was six and one-half years before the Wright brothers and Kitty Hawk. The reports covered a period of two days, from April 17 through 18, and quote many eyewitnesses from a nine-county radius. This would appear, on the surface, to give some weight to at least the possibility that something out of the ordinary was in the air of that long-ago April.

But it doesn't really.

One has only to read the stories to realize that what was in the air that Aries was a happy contagion of cosmic invention that caught the fancy of every village Jules Verne.

The communications of that day were not so primitive that a good joke like this could not make its rounds. Railroad telegraphers and drummers passed it from town to town, papers picked it up and printed it, and pretty soon everybody with any wit was in on it.

In Stephenville, out in Erath County, C. L. McIlhany, a farmer, talked to the crew (two men) after the "aerial monster" landed in his pasture. Mr. McIlhany's imagination, alas, was not as lofty—as far out—as our own Mr. Haydon's. His airmen were not from Mars, but that other weird place, New York, and they were only testing the world's first "aeroplane," a cigar-shaped contraption powered by electrically charged windmill fans. That was on April 17.

The next day, over in Waxahachie, in Ellis County, a Judge Love of that city had a similar experience, only this time the crewmen were long-lost Jews from the ten tribes of Israel. Since

Biblical times they had been living in the North Pole; they had learned English from the explorers Sir Hugh Willoughby and Sir John Franklin and were on their way to the centennial exhibition in Nashville to show off their airships.

On the stories soared, taking rarified forms, until Dr. E. Etuart of Ennis, Ellis County's foremost metaphysicist, declared in the *Morning News* that the whole affair was due to hypnotism and bad whiskey.

Here in Wise County, on this caliche hill, the tale of the flying panatella, as Jerry Flemmons calls it, must have been as refreshing to S. E. Haydon and J. S. Proctor as the promise of rail service had been a few years earlier. Both were men of some substance, at least in character and leadership. They had staked their future on Aurora and had seen it boom and then, within a decade, wither before their eyes. Decatur got the county seat and courthouse and the Bible college, Bridgeport got the coal mines, Boyd got the Rock Island line and Rhome the Ft. Worth & Denver. And Aurora? So named for the luminosity of its morning dawns? Well, all Aurora got were the boll weevil, a disastrous downtown fire, and two fever epidemics that sent most of its citizenry to the cemetery, or in flight to other towns. By 1897 it was a ghost of its former self.

Yet Judge Proctor stood fast, because his family had been there since before the Civil War and because he was the justice of the peace. Haydon hung around because his wife and sons were in the graveyard, victims of the fever. What sustained them, this old judge and this cotton man, we now realize, was a sense of humor.

We can see it, this jauntiness in the face of adversity, in the only photograph left of Mr. Haydon. It was taken at a local cotton gin. There must be a dozen or so men milling around on the ground. But Haydon stands out from the rest. He's the one posing atop the cotton bale, his thumbs in his vest, head and shoulders above the rest.

Loren Eisely once wrote that "vast desolation and a kind of absence in nature invite the emergence of equally strange beings or spectacular natural events," and I think that's what happened in the desolation that was Aurora back in 1897.

The spaceman came to Aurora, and Haydon and Judge Proctor had some laughs. Some relief. Can't you see them cooking it up and Haydon riding into the telegraph office in Rhome to file it with the papers?

Mrs. Robbie Reynolds Hanson was a girl of twelve at the time, and she remembers that Judge Proctor ran his own version, similar to Haydon's but in the judge's words, in the little local paper he published, a two-sheeter called the *Aurora News*.

Mrs. Hanson talks about how her father, J. D. Reynolds, the town constable, read Judge Proctor's "joke" in the Aurora paper and roared with laughter. "The judge has really outdone himself this time," the constable said. Mrs. Hanson remembers it clearly because it was around her birthday. No one took the spaceman story seriously. The judge and Haydon were known to be men who liked to tease, and both wrote satirical essays and poems for the local paper.

Mrs. Hanson is not the only native who is astonished, and a little put out, that anyone would take the legend of the Aurora spaceman as Galilean gospel.

Yet I, too, in a sense, have taken it seriously, as a marvelous *human* story worth retelling.

The extraterrestrial part of it Bill Case and Dr. Hynek can have.

It isn't that I believe that man is at center stage in the universe and that there is no room for other beings. That would be presumptuous. I am as open to the unexpected nature of the cosmos as any man. It is just that I have a greater appreciation of the reality of those two good rogues, Judge Proctor and Mr. Haydon, than I do of the riddle they left us.

The answer doesn't lie at this wellhead, but with them, wherever they are.

I wish I could tell you where indeed they are—their earthly remains, I mean—and what fate dealt them. But I can't. They seem to have disappeared, to have lost themselves, perhaps on purpose, perhaps the better to grin and bear our interminable intruding "science."

Aurora, 1973

Farewell to LBJ:
A Hill Country Valediction

1

Never in memory had the hill winter been so hard and insistent and the sun so shy. Men talked of it on the town squares as they backed up to stoves and toasted their behinds. It wasn't idle talk of weather, but the real thing, as if some elemental malevolence was in the air. Twice an icy sheet had covered the whole of Texas, and out here in these runty ruins of some ancient geologic upheaval, young and old counted a dreary run of coughs and colds and linament-filled nights.

He, of course, had not died of pneumonia, being too robust for that. Like strong men do, he had been up one day, planting trees, and was gone the next. He had died of a turbulence inside himself that had nothing to do with the weather.

That day of his burial we all looked to the sky, and the sun tried to show itself, kept poking here and there through the pall over the Twin Sister Mountains, giving rise to all kinds of false hopes and comment in the people about.

The matriarch of the Johnson clan was Aunt Jessie Hermine Johnson Hatcher, at eighty-eight the ninth and last surviving child of grandfather Sam Ealy Johnson, Sr. Now there was never any question about Aunt Jessie's attendance at the graveside services. The doughty old girl would be there to see her Lyndon off. The prayer was that she would not catch her death of cold.

2

The petition on Red Casparis's chapped lips was that he could wet a few whistles before George Byars's proclamation went into effect. George, being the mayor of Johnson City, had deemed it proper that business establishments close for the funeral, so Red got up early that dark Thursday to try to sneak a little daylight by the rooster that would crow on curfew.

It isn't that Red is a crassly commercial man; he couldn't be and keep the kind of saloon he does on the square behind the courthouse. All he sells is beer. It is about as private a club as goat ropers can have. And innocent, I thought. You never see any women in there, and the male mainstays seem to be Red and Ted and Austin, Casparises all, Pancho Althaus, the barber, and Lyndon Johnson's common cousin, James Ealy. Ted is Red's cousin, and Austin is Red's daddy. Austin is ninety-four. Austin and his late wife, Fannie, used to serve Lyndon chili a lot when they had a café and he was a kid, so I asked Red if the old man would make it to the cemetery. He smiled and said he doubted it.

"Like to," he allowed in his gravelly whisper, "Sure, daddy'd like to, but he's a little under the weather, too much to drink last night. Yessir, he put one on."

As I left, Red had lit the stove and was, with a feather duster in hand and an appreciative smile on his round, rich face, carefully examining and dusting what he called his Texas primitives, a rusty assortment of odds and ends he had found in the ruins of barns and had artfully arranged about the walls of his joint.

It was hard to imagine the authorities closing him down from time to time for fights and trouble there. Hell, who would be fighting? Not Red, and surely not Ted. Behind the Falstaff fog, or whatever brand of balm he used, Ted Casparis was a man of mind who hid behind his war wounds. The barber was a good-humored man, well known and respected. Old Austin was out of the question, and as for James Ealy, well, heck, he wasn't that ambitious. It had to be some out-of-town tush hogs. Damn shame what a little boom like the presidency will do to the old home town.

The air was a damp fist in the face as I walked out Red's door and stumbled over a dog that had taken shelter there. The mutt whined and shivered, its thin legs as veined as thermometers. Rain. It had begun again, the kind of drizzle that gives grave diggers a bailing-out fit. Down the street the mercury on Pancho's barber pole was just a little above freezing.

Sure, I thought, he had his fat-butted cronies in boots, greed, and gabardine, but he also had Roosevelt and Rayburn.

3

By noon everything in Johnson City was shut down, even the cafés out on the highway, and by one o'clock a steady stream of cars began heading out Highway 290 toward Stonewall and the LBJ Ranch, where, in the old family cemetery beside the Pedernales, he would be placed beside his mother and daddy. The ceremony was not to start until four o'clock, when Lyndon's body would be flown in from the state funeral at the cathedral in Washington. But the impulse, in spite of the cold, was to hurry to the cemetery and get a good spot before the crush came. What you did if you were an ordinary citizen was park your car in the LBJ State Park on Ranch Road 1 south of the Johnson place and catch one of the army shuttle buses that took you across the river and into the trees that hung like mourners over the huddle of tombstones. Thousands did this, or walked the winding road to the graveyard, where they stood in puddles for hours awaiting his last trip home. What you did if you were the press was sign in at the park office and get a badge which gave you precedence over the run-of-the-mill mourner for a bus and a front-row position. Still the press bitched, because the dignitaries were given reserved seats on exclusive buses, because there were only nine phones for calling out, because it was wet and cold and difficult to set men and machinery into motion.

4

Sam Wood, the veteran Austin editor, was in a better humor than most. He sat in one of the shuttle buses beside his reporter, Nat Henderson, his head down in a deep study. Directly he looked up and out at the clouds. "Say," he said to Henderson, "I'll bet you ten dollars it stops raining and the sun comes out."

"Why?"

"Because," Wood chuckled, "Saint Peter doesn't know what he's up against."

Lyndon would have loved that.

The little rotund Lutheran pastor, Wunibald Schneider, was of the same mind, only in his German way much more earnest about the theological import of rain or shine. He stepped out of his church across the river from the cemetery and looked up for a sign, for some show of a benign and benevolent benediction on what was about to transpire.

I doubt Lyndon would have liked that. If the sun had come out it probably would have scared hell out of him.

5

How would you rank him as a president? One of the best. Between ninth and twelfth, I think, somewhere in there among Grover Cleveland, James K. Polk, and Dwight Eisenhower. That's what I would tell Saul when we got back to Austin and the Villa Capri. It would enrage him, I knew. I hadn't seen Saul Friedman in years, but he'd never liked LBJ. But I'd hold to it, warts and the war and all.

6

Word came that the body would not arrive by plane at the airstrip on the ranch, but was being brought by hearse from Austin, down 290 through Oak Hill and Dripping Springs and Henly, Johnson City, and Hye. I looked at Bo Byers's watch: 3:15. Wally Pryor said the entourage was now passing through Oak Hill, less than an hour away. Was it sudden sentiment to have him brought by car along that road he had known so well? Whatever, I approved, and thought of the places along the way, the people I knew who might watch the procession pass. Dick Polk, the calf-roping, guitar-picking, gas-jockeying postmaster and feed man at Oak Hill. At Henly, if they knew, maybe the twin sisters who had married brothers would be out on their porches. That would be Ella Mae and Hazel Herbest, who had got the Smitherman boys. Hondo Crouch wouldn't be at Hye but at Luckenbach.

7

Wayne Jackson and I were crunched up against the low stone wall that rectangled the cemetery, but we made room for Ronnie Dugger. The rest of the reporters were exchanging stories, but Ronnie remained quiet. I wondered what sense he would make of it. For years he had been coming to grips with Lyndon Johnson, mostly in the *Texas Observer*. Now he was writing a book about Johnson, had been for some time. Dugger is a discerning man, mentally quick on his feet but deliberate and philosophical in print, and since the fifties he had quarreled with most that Johnson had stood for. Saul came up, and we asked Ronnie to join us later at the Villa Capri.

It really wasn't hard to understand the Texas liberals' long war with Lyndon. On the Potomac he may have made like FDR with his programs for the poor, but down here on the Pedernales he ran with men who put more money in a fat steer than they would in a house full of starving Mexicans.

8

I looked at the hole they would lower him into and wondered if he had ever heard of the Smithermans. I doubted it, though he must have passed their place hundreds of times over the past fifty-five years. Of course they knew him, as obscure and modest neighbors know a great and public figure, but they also knew him better than that implies. Part of it, I figured, had to do with the presidency itself. For the Smithermans and for most Americans, I felt, there was still a magic in that office. Yes, because of its incredible and growing power, but also because it was, in Clinton Rossiter's words, "a breeding ground of indestructible myth." As soon as a man stepped into that office he became a flesh-and-blood democratic distillation of us all. If we loved and hated him, it was because we loved and hated ourselves. And there was no question about it. Lyndon Johnson had engendered those extremes. Why, I asked myself, when I thought of LBJ I always thought of old D and Jody and Jesse?

They had moved into Blanco County back in the summer

of '27, just a few months after Lyndon had left for college. He had gone off to San Marcos with seventy-five dollars in borrowed money, a hell of a lot less than D and Jody and Jesse had brought with them. Why, they had something like two thousand head of cattle, which they pastured on a 1,280-acre lease along Flat Creek.

Funny how things turn out.

For the next thirty-six years—the time it took Lyndon to rise to the presidency—D and Jody and Jesse wore themselves to a frazzle trying to make a living out there on what has to be the sorriest land since Terlingua. While Lyndon had gone from student to teacher to congressional secretary to bureaucrat to congressman, senator, vice-president, and president, the Smithermans had gone from two thousand cows to less than fifty, from one thousand acres to three hundred. Why, they'd even gone to sheep and goats, which made them beyond redemption as far as cowmen were concerned. About the only thing sassy they managed to bring off was marrying sisters—Jody and Jesse, that is; D never married. Jody finally removed himself from the partnership, and he and Hazel moved into Henly. Out on the ranch, fat D spent most of his time trying to coax fig trees out of the caliche and limestone, and out in the barn frail Jesse was always raising a racket inventing contraptions like self-feeders and hayloft lifts which never got off the place. And all the time Lyndon Johnson was making millions and moving in high cotton. Did they give him hell like J. Evetts Haley? Were they bitter? When he passed on the road in his Lincoln did they cuss? Why hell no, D told me one day as he fried a sausage patty to a black crisp, it was nice to see somebody get ahead. And when he became president, it kind of perked them up.

Ella Mae, Jesse's wife, started melting down beer bottles, which she made into LBJ ashtrays to sell to tourists.

Jesse commenced to talk seriously about putting in a barbecue stand on Highway 290. Why, it was bound to be a money maker. It looked like Lyndon was going to be president for nine years, and if he wasn't the best advertisement for barbecue and beer, Jesse didn't know one. Might even put in a motel. Ella

Mae could sell her ceramics, and D could do the cooking. Jesse got so excited he poked a finger into D's chest. "I'll tell you somethin' else," he declared. "We ought to think about gettin' some Holstein cows, some milkers." He knew damn good and well people were going to keep on drinking milk. By God, the country was beginning to look up with Lyndon in there.

Well, none of it came to pass.

Not the Great Society.

Not the nine years.

Oh, Ella Mae sold a few ashtrays, but not from any Smitherman Bros. Barbecue Stand.

Jesse got sick and died, and that was that.

D, in his seventies, had no heart for it or for the milkers.

And when Ella Mae got glaucoma and had to have two eye operations, she stopped melting down beer bottles.

I spent a few hours with them, the widow and the bachelor, one day back in January, 1969, shortly after Lyndon Johnson had called it quits to retire to the ranch. Ella Mae hadn't missed her ceramics. "It's a small thing to have to give up after losing a husband," she said. "Just look what Lyndon's given up."

And we did look, for there on the television screen was Richard M. Nixon, taking the oath as thirty-seventh president.

The inauguration saddened them, not because they had anything against Nixon, but because they felt so sorry for Lyndon Johnson.

"I know that seems a silly thing to say," Ella Mae said, "especially when you consider how far he has gone in the world, and from such a little place like Johnson City! But I feel for him and I can't help it. The country turned crazy on him, and he had to step down to save it. People don't seem to appreciate that."

9

D Smitherman died in April, 1972. I knew that as I stood next to the cemetery wall. But I did not know that at that moment Jody Smitherman lay in a San Antonio hospital trying to make it back from a heart attack. As Hazel was to put it, "They helicoptered him there just ahead of Lyndon."

10

Now, just behind Lyndon, after the hearse that bore his body, came the family in limousines, and after the family came friends and business associates in limousines, and after them came buses, many buses, unloading important people, many of whom we recognized—Hubert Humphrey, Ed Muskie—but most of whom were VIP's of the Texas establishment who had not made it to Washington for the more formal services. Anyone who was anybody or who wanted to be was there.

One fair young man caught my eye in the forest of great-coats. Although he stood taller than the men around him, he was somehow subdued and lacking in stature. Perhaps it was what I knew of Ben Barnes that gave him this rather contra-dictory diminution.

The man whose body the military pallbearers were carry-ing now to the grave had singled out this young man as his po-litical son, had coached and counseled and favored him to the point that everyone said it was a matter of time before Barnes would be governor and maybe president. It was said that the mantle of greatness had been laid upon him. But just as the young man made his first big move, he stumbled, badly, and the people turned from him. I looked at him now and won-dered if the men who used to buoy him up had also left him like a leper. I had never thought much of him myself, but now he fascinated me. He was becoming either a very wise man or a very bitter one, depending upon his inner character, and the latter, of course, had never come to light in the days of his pub-lic apprenticeship.

11

Before that particular young man had been favored by the departed, another had been his favorite from the time they had been novices in the pursuit of power. Now he came, tall and handsome in his maturity, to eulogize the dead man. And surely the common thought—it caught your breath—was that here, embodied in both, might well be the once and future kings.

12

At one point in his eulogy, John Connally quoted Lyndon Johnson as having said, "I guess I've come a long way for a boy from Johnson City, Texas." Certainly Connally had come a long way himself, but I couldn't help but think, as we watched him read over his friend, that the truly stunning turn in his life was not the years between the Floresville farm and the governor's mansion, but rather those of late.

Who would have thought, say, in 1960, when John Kennedy and Lyndon Johnson sent Richard Nixon and Henry Cabot Lodge to the sidelines and beckoned Mr. Connally to Washinton as their secretary of the navy, that it would be President Nixon, not President Kennedy or President Johnson, who would set John Connally up for a run at the White House? Not even our knowledge then that Connally was a counterfeit Democrat would have prepared us for such a turn of events.

13

Maybe that was premature, putting Connally in the White House when we still had a Texas president to put in the ground. Well, what of him, this Lyndon Johnson who yet made such sounds in the earth? The Graham cracker generalities that the Reverend Billy Graham was serving up over his grave did not hit home. What occurred to me then (and I hold to it now) is that not since Andrew Jackson had a president contained such an abundance of both virtue and flaw. In his character and manner and sympathies, Lyndon Johnson was in that great rough-hewn line of succession that began with Old Hickory and found such full expression in our towering genius Abraham Lincoln. It was passed down, in part, to Theodore Roosevelt and then to Truman, this rude kind of humanity, but of all of them, LBJ was the closest to Jackson.

It doesn't surprise me that Jackson's great friend and spiritual brother was Sam Houston. If Houston was a colossus in buckskin, LBJ was the colossus in khaki. It is uncanny how alike they were. Houston was in Texas because of President Jackson's bidding, and their intent was empire. Sam Houston came to Texas on borrowed money and made a pot while becoming president of the Republic. His sins were human ones. Lyndon Johnson went to Washington on borrowed money and made a pot while becoming president of the United States. His sins were human ones.

They wanted everything, and they went out and got it— power, money, land, a place in history among the titans. Everything but love in their own time and on their own terms.

Both Houston and Johnson were larger-than-life incarnations of Western Man. They believed, by God and by their own prowess and passions, that everything was possible in this world. Chaotic men of massive contradictions, they ruled with rage as well as reason and left in their wake both good fortune and calamity.

Both fell from power because the people turned against them, Houston for trying to prevent a war, Johnson for pursuing one. Both retired from the public arena with heavy hearts and died, if not in disrepute, then in disregard.

14

The way we stood in concentric circles about the casket reminded me of the circles of life in a fallen oak, with the dead man our common core. The first influences on Lyndon Johnson had been those of his hill country boyhood, but as he grew they receded from his center toward the bark of his background, to make room for each succeeding stage of his life. And indeed, the "plain people," as John Connally called them, were at our backs, making a great outward circle of several thousand persons. In front of them, in a smaller circumference, were the politicians he had known in his middle stage, and in front of them were those who had served him in the White House. And at the heart of the goodbyes, of course, were the old friends and business associates and the kin.

A fifth circle was wedged in as close to the family as the stone wall and the secret service would allow: the press, rapacious and rude in its appetite for one final insight and intimacy into the man and what he had meant.

15

History redeemed Houston.

We tended to think of Johnson as a consummate politician, but I wonder. Of course he was with the boys in the back rooms of Congress. He came to rule the Senate as no man in our history. If it hadn't been for Senator Johnson and his majority whip and carrot, Eisenhower would have been left out on the fairway.

But God, was he a bore on the podium, speechmaking! Somebody's middle-class Masonic uncle, beaming a benign conservatism through his bifocals, when you knew damn well he had just broken somebody's back for crossing him. Up close, pressing your flesh and looking you in the eye, or at his leisure with a Pearl beer in one hand (Jesse was right) and a barbecued rib in the other, he was as winning as John Wayne.

The cinematic Wayne, not the new nominating one. He's as dull on the podium as Johnson was.

As Billy Graham.

16

Lady Bird and her girls bore up beautifully, Lynda in her proud, Protestant singing along with Anita Bryant (who was magnificent), and Lucy in her Catholic quiet.

But the old aunts, Aunt Jessie Hatcher in particular, you could tell were chilled to the bone.

17

He was a genius in the Senate, gloried in it.

The presidency was something else. I don't think he ever felt quite at home there, never really hit his stride. Like Andrew Johnson after Lincoln and Chester A. Arthur after James Garfield, he came to it sadly, with a nation in tears. Jack Kennedy had been so beautifully young and vibrant.

But after a time he made it his, came into his own enough to pass the most comprehensive and far-reaching civil rights legislation of any president. In this he was a second Lincoln. He put into law what Lincoln had dreamed of and what Kennedy had schemed of. What he did for the minorities was the high mark of his five years in the White House.

But it was not legislation calculated to make him a popular president. In this he led the people and the Congress instead of following. Our inclination as a people was toward racial injustice, and had Lyndon Johnson been a weaker man, it would have been easier to ignore the militants and go along with the country's prevailing opinion. But he saw the light, and the right, though it was against our grain. The irony, and it was a bitter pill for Johnson to swallow, was that not even the black people loved him for it.

Our mood, as a people, was contentious, as it was in Jackson's time, in Lincoln's time, and we barked and bit at Johnson, and at one another, like dogs.

It was not consensus, but contention, and he was miserable and must have commiserated with the ghosts of past presidents. Now he knew why Washington had left the presidency sore in heart and mind, eager for the seclusion of Mount Vernon. Jefferson had called the presidency the road to splendid misery, and Jackson had sworn it more curse than honor.

That was what Vietnam was for Lyndon Johnson. More curse than honor was his Waterloo, and it doesn't take history's long view to see how tragically absurd his position was. Here, on the one hand, he was pouring manpower and billions of dollars into the making of our own Great Society, while on the other he was waging one of the longest and costliest wars in our history, not against a major power, but on a tiny country and in support of a corrupt regime.

It is true he inherited the commitment from Kennedy and the policy of containment from Truman, but he let both get away from him. He paid for it, and we are still paying for it.

18

The twenty-one-cannon salute fell short by two. A howitzer misfired twice.

19

It hurt me to think back over his last lame-duck days in the White House. No president since James Polk had worked harder and enjoyed it less. He had wanted to take the country by the tail, but, gargantuan that he was, he reached for more than he could handle.

But great men always do. Because, I guess, they are metaphors for the best and worst in all of us.

20

Red sold four beers all that morning.

Dugger never did make it to the Capri, and Saul and I talked of Nixon.

Neither did Jody make it out of the hospital. Hazel said he died two weeks later.

So did Aunt Jessie Hatcher, two weeks to the day. She caught a cold, and it went into pneumonia. They buried her in the same cemetery.

Johnson City, 1973

The articles listed below have been previously published, some under different titles or in slightly different form, in the following publications:

Chicago Daily News
"Barrymore of the Courtroom"

D, the Magazine of Dallas
"Uncle John"
"The Outcasts of Western Heights Cemetery"
"The Ghost of Amon Carter"
"The Last Spring of Our Innocence"
"On the Banks with Larry Bowman"

Du Pont *Context*
"Introduction: A Mythical Place"

Houston Chronicle
"Old Juan"
"Clarence of Green Mansions"
"The Folk Singer Who Sang Opera"
"The Stone That Cries Like a Child"
"Don Pedrito"
"Ravel's Elegy and the Sad Violinist"
"The Sanctified Lady"

Texas Monthly
"Farewell to LBJ: A Hill Country Valediction"
"The Cowboy"
"The Santa Berta"
"The New Ranchers"
"An Oilman"
"H. L. Hunt's Long Good-bye"

Texas Observer
"J. D. and the Gang in The Grove"
"The Genius"
"The Aurora Spaceman"
"The Christian and the Pagan"